VIRTUES OF JERUSALEM

VIRTUES *of* JERUSALEM

An Islamic Perspective

فضائل القدس

ISMAIL ADAM PATEL

AL-AQSA PUBLISHERS

Published by
Al-Aqsa Publishers,
PO Box 5127,
Leicester LE2 0WU,
United Kingdom
e-mail: info@aqsa.org.uk
website: www.aqsa.org.uk
Tel: 07711 823524, Fax: ++ 44 (116) 253 7575

British Library Cataloguing-in-Publication Data
Patel, Ismail Adam
Virtues of Jerusalem: an Islamic Perspective
1. Jerusalem in Islam
I. Title
297.3'5569442

ISBN –10: 0-9536530-2-1

ISBN –13: 978-0-9536530-2-1

Cover Design by: Aziz ul Hoque
Printed and bound in England by Antony Rowe Ltd, Chippenham, Wiltshire

Contents

Transliteration Table iv
Introduction v

1. The Qur'ān 1
2. A Blessed and Holy Land 3
3. The Place and Direction of Worship 10
4. Through Symbolic Expression 20
5. Through Seasonal Expression 22
6. Prophets and People 23
7. Through Events 53
8. A Place of Migration 67
9. A Place of Struggle 70
10. The Centre of Belief and Goodness 72
11. A Place of Caliphate 74
12. The Virtues of Praying and Charity 76
13. Travel for Prayers 80
14. Starting Ḥajj or 'Umrah From Masjid al-Aqṣā 82
15. Historical Significance 84
16. Prophesied and Land of Promise 105
17. Guide and Plan of al-Ḥaram al-Sharīf 108

Notes 136
Appendix 138
Qur'ānic References 138
Index 143

Transliteration Table

Consonants. Arabic

initial: unexpressed medial and final:

ء	ʾ	د	d	ض	ḍ	ك	k
ب	b	ذ	dh	ط	ṭ	ل	l
ت	t	ر	r	ظ	ẓ	م	m
ث	th	ز	z	ع	ʿ	ن	n
ج	j	س	s	غ	gh	هـ	h
ح	ḥ	ش	sh	ف	f	و	w
خ	kh	ص	ṣ	ق	q	ي	y

Vowels, diphthongs, etc.

short:	ـَ	a	ـِ	i	ـُ	u
long:	ـَا	ā	ـِي	ī	ـُو	ū
diphthongs:			ـَوْ	aw		
			ـَىْ	ay		

Introduction

AL-ḤARAM AL-SHARĪF (al-Aqṣā Sanctuary) is the holiest site in al-Quds (Jerusalem); a place used for worship, residence and meditation by many Prophets and pious individuals, past and present. It is a site blessed by Allah ﷻ and made to be one of the most holy areas on earth, where angels descended with Allah's message to chosen Prophets.

It was also the site of the most fantastic and incredible journey undertaken by the Prophet Muḥammad ﷺ during the night of al-Isrā' and al-Mi'rāj, when he was taken up to the heavens by the command of Allah ﷻ. The revered site of al-Aqṣā Sanctuary was also the first *qiblah* in Islam, before Allah ﷻ inspired the Prophet ﷺ to change it to the Holy Masjid in Makkah.

The Holy Sanctuary of al-Aqṣā saw the second house of Allah ﷻ, after the Ka'bah built by Prophet Ādam عليه السلام on earth. This was also the place to where Prophet Ibrāhīm عليه السلام migrated and lived for most of his life. Here, Ibrāhīm عليه السلام lived and traded, taught the Tawḥīd of Allah ﷻ, re-built the Masjid within the sanctuary of al-Aqṣā and finally passed away. The grave of Prophet Ibrāhīm عليه السلام is in a place near al-Aqṣā Sanctuary called al-Khalīl (Hebron).

This is where Ya'qūb (Jacob) عليه السلام raised his twelve sons and from where Yūsuf (Joseph) عليه السلام was taken and sold in Egypt as a slave child. A few centuries later, Mūsā (Moses) ﵇ was directed by Allah ﷾ to migrate from Egypt with the descendants of Ya'qūb ﵇ and travel back to al-Quds (Jerusalem). After the flight from the Pharaoh, Mūsā ﵇ travelled across the desert with his people and prayed to the Almighty that he would prefer to be at a place near al-Aqṣā Sanctuary when overtaken by death.

Dāwūd (David) ﵇ was from the people of Mūsā ﵇ and after conquering the city of al-Quds (Jerusalem), he spent a great deal of time in al-Aqṣā Sanctuary meditating and with the power of Allah ﷾ the very hills of the glorious city of al-Quds celebrated the praises of the Almighty with Dāwūd ﵇: "*the hills declare in unison with him (Dāwūd) Our Praises, at evening and at break of day, and the birds gathered all with him did turn to Allah*" (38: 18-19). The private chamber of Dāwūd ﵇ mentioned in the Qur'ān was within al-Aqṣā Sanctuary: "*has the story of the disputants reached you. Behold, they climbed over the wall of the private chamber*" (38: 21).

The son of Dāwūd ﵇, Sulaymān (Solomon) ﵇ resided in al-Quds and was granted a great kingdom there due to his righteousness. The wind was made subject to him, enabling him to fly above and beyond al-Quds. Sulaymān ﵇ completed the building of the Masjid al-Aqṣā within al-Ḥaram al-Sharīf which his father, Prophet Dāwūd ﵇ had begun.

Arāmiyah (Jeremia) ﵇ preached at al-Aqṣā Sanctuary and worked towards bringing the divergent and divided tribes of Banū Isrā'īl towards Tawḥīd. It was during his era that Nebuchadnezzar, the King of Babylon invaded the city, destroyed all the buildings within al-Aqṣā Sanctuary and levelled the whole city of al-Quds (Jerusalem) to the ground.

In later times, Zakariyā ﵇ was the Imām of the Masjid al-Aqṣā and he supplicated to the Almighty Allah ﷾ for a son: "*there did Zakariyā pray to his Lord, saying, my Lord, grant me a child who is pure...*" (3: 38). The very Sanctuary of al-Aqṣā is where Sayyidatunā Maryam, the mother of 'Īsā (Jesus) ﵇ meditated and worshipped Allah ﷾. This is also the place where the angels brought the glad tidings to Sayyidatunā Maryam about the miraculous conception and birth of ʻĪsā ﷺ.

These are some of the many major incidents that took place around al-Aqṣā Sanctuary and ensured its high and lofty status in the hearts of Muslims throughout the centuries. To reflect their devotions, Muslims of previous generations have constructed the most fantastic places of worship within al-Aqṣā Sanctuary. They have maintained it by investing their wealth, energy and resources and, when it was required, they gave their lives to protect al-Aqṣā Sanctuary.

The Holy city of al-Quds (Jerusalem) is referred to by several names. The Byzantines named it *Ilyā' Capitolina, Ilyā'* for short, after one of their gods. Muslims refer to it as: *Bayt al-Maqdis, al-Quds* and *Madīnat al-Salām*, which means the "city of peace". Bayt al-Maqdis meaning "the house of purity or purification" is the name that is reported in various traditions of the Prophet Muḥammad ﷺ and used by his Companions. It is referred to as the "house of purification" because it is a place where attempts have been made to purify mankind and raise human beings to a greater level of consciousness by the many Prophets who lived there preaching Allah's message. Al-Quds means "the purest place". Al-Quds is the most popular term used today by Muslims and Christian Arabs.

The city of al-Quds (Jerusalem) now extends over an area of 45 square km. Within al-Quds is the 'old city' where major historical events took place and within the old city on the southeast corner is the area referred to as al-Ḥaram al-Sharīf or al-Aqṣā Sanctuary. Al-Aqṣā Sanctuary covers an area of approximately 35 acres and within this area, at the southern end, is the black domed Masjid called Masjid al-Aqṣā; in the centre lies the golden domed Masjid, Qubbat al-Ṣakhrah (Dome of the Rock) and there are within al-Aqṣā Sanctuary, 42 other monuments and buildings. It has become common practice to refer to the whole area simply as al-Ḥaram al-Sharīf (al-Aqṣā Sanctuary) and the black domed Masjid as Masjid al-Aqṣā.

However, it is important to be aware of the distinction between the al-Aqṣā Sanctuary and Masjid al-Aqṣā. It is extremely important to appreciate that it is the land of al-Ḥaram al-Sharīf (al-Aqṣā Sanctuary) that is the most precious and blessed. When the Holy Qur'ān (in *Sūrah al-Isrā'*) refers to Masjid al-Aqṣā (meaning a place of prostration) it is this land of al-Ḥaram al-Sharīf (al-Aqṣā Sanctuary) that is implied and not any of the buildings. Although the buildings within the noble sanctuary, like the black domed Masjid al-Aqṣā and gold domed Dome of the Rock (Qubbat al-Ṣakhrah) are of great historical significance, however, one must understand that it is the land that is holy and blessed and not the bricks and mortar.

The glorious Dome of the Rock (Qubbat al-Ṣakhrah) captivates the landscape of al-Quds (Jerusalem) and has done so for hundreds of years, a testimony of Muslims' devotion to al-Aqṣā Sanctuary. The great and beautiful black domed Mosque called Masjid al-Aqṣā can house over five thousand worshippers. In recent years the re-opening of the Muṣallā Marwānī quarters has maintained the tradition of looking after al-Aqṣā Sanctuary, even in adversity and under occupation.

The love and sacrifice of the pious predecessors indicates the importance and centrality of al-Aqṣā Sanctuary. However, there are healthy theological debates on whether al-Aqṣā Sanctuary is a "Ḥaram" or not. The various views include: Al-Shafi'ī (raḥimahullāh) and al-Shawkānī (raḥimahullāh), who regard al-Aqṣā as a Ḥaram but others think only Makkah and Madinah are the Ḥaramayn. Yet other scholars consider only Makkah to be the Ḥaram. Regardless of its status as Ḥaram or not, no one can dispute the great virtues, blessings and holiness of al-Aqṣā Sanctuary. The debate in no way undermines the eminence and the deep central position al-Aqṣā Sanctuary has carved within the psyche of the Muslim Ummah and formed the nucleus of one of the most Holy sites on earth.

Above and beyond these great events and personalities associated with al-Aqṣā Sanctuary which brings to the fore glorious memories of Prophets and miraculous events, one can never forget that Masjid al-Aqṣā is mentioned by name in the Holy Qur'ān. Further, Almighty Allah ﷻ refers to the region of al-Aqṣā Sanctuary as blessed and holy.

Unfortunately, the general malaise that has recently set in within some quarters has had an unconscious impact upon the love and devotion we need to shower upon al-Aqṣā Sanctuary. Coincidentally, this is also one of the bleakest periods in the history of al-Aqṣā Sanctuary, where not only the structural buildings within it are in danger of being physically destroyed but the whole of al-Aqṣā Sanctuary is threatened with occupation and removal from Muslim hands.

Over the past centuries, Muslims have toiled with their wealth and lives to ensure that suceeding generations inherit the glory of al-Aqṣā Sanctuary. This drive seems to have evaporated from many within this present generation. Love for the symbols of Islam, which is a testimony of piety, is lacking within Muslims and consequently al-Aqṣā Sanctuary faces its greatest danger.

It is my ardent hope, and I supplicate to Allah ﷻ, that my fellow Muslims will, after reading this book, build love and affection for and strive to safeguard al-Aqṣā Sanctuary by whatever way and means possible to them.

I humbly request the Imāms and individuals responsible for running Mosques to make it a routine of spending two minutes in reciting a ḥādīth, explaining a verse of the Qur'ān or reading a paragraph from this book after one of the *farḍ* ṣalāh each day. We pray through the Mercy of Allah ﷻ that our effort will be accepted and a new generation of Muslims will grow with sincere devotion to al-Aqṣā Sanctuary, as it rightly deserves.

The noble sanctuary of al-Aqṣā and al-Quds are referred to directly and indirectly over 70 times in the Holy Qur'ān. Qur'ānic references are categorised in small chapters within this book for ease of reference and for a clearer appreciation of the importance of al-Aqṣā Sanctuary. Chapters 1 to 7 detail Qur'ānic references to the nature of al-Aqṣā Sanctuary as: A Blessed and Holy Land; The Place and Direction of Worship; Through Symbolic Expression; Through Seasonal Expression; Prophets and People; Through Events.

Wherever possible, aḥādīth accompany Qur'ānic references. Chapters 8 to 14 are in essence a continuation of the virtues but mainly cover aḥādīth as source material detailing the importance of al-Aqṣā Sanctuary by virtue of its role as: A Place of Migration; A Place of Struggle; The Centre of Belief and Goodness; A Place of Caliphate; Virtues of Praying and Charity; Travel for Prayers; Starting Ḥajj or 'Umrah from Masjid al-Aqṣā.

Chapter 15 summarises the historical events that relate to al-Quds and al-Aqṣā Sanctuary. Chapter 16 is Prophesied and Land of Promise. Finally, chapter 17 shows a Site Plan and Guide to al-Ḥaram al-Sharīf to assist travellers around the noble sanctuary of al-Aqṣā.

I am grateful to Brother Ibrahim Hewitt, who despite the burden of his own work, helped me with the proofreading; Abu Qasim Spiker for providing me with pictures of 4 buildings within al-Aqṣā Sanctuary; Sister Nasreen Ibrahim and Maulana Abdulhafiz Qadir, Abu Idris and Abu Mustafa for the typesetting; to my wife and children, Mariam, Huzayfa and Humayra who excused me from their needs. I pray for them and many friends and colleagues who have assisted me in bringing this book to publication. I humbly request the reader to remember me in their du'ā'.

Leicester, UK
Sha'bān 1427
August 2006

1 The Qur'ān

THE HOLY QUR'ĀN is the Word of the Creator and was sent as guidance to the "whole of mankind". It calls humanity to the natural way of living, "*to think*" and surrender to the Creator, Allah ﷻ.

Those who submit to the natural way and have surrendered to the Will of the Creator, are called Muslims. For them, the Holy Qur'ān is the medium which attaches them to the Lord, Allah ﷻ.

Hence, what is within the Qur'ān forms the basic and fundamental aspect of a person's knowledge of Islām, which they must study, understand and practise.

Practising upon the verses of the Qur'ān is the basis upon which one acquires awareness and consciousness of Allah ﷻ and is called *taqwā*. Every letter and word that makes up the Holy Qur'ān must be dear to a believer and to waver on any aspect of the Qur'ān nullifies one's claim to be a Muslim. As it is the requirement of a Muslim to adhere to the lawful and prohibited within the Qur'ān, it is equally important to show reverence to and extol the virtues of the "symbols of Islam": "*... Whoever holds in honour the Symbols of Allah, such honour is an indication of the piety of heart*" (22: 32). If the need arises one has to be prepared to defend these "symbols" as they form the basic requirement of a believer.

The importance and virtues of al-Aqṣā Sanctuary can be gauged by the fact that Masjid al-Aqṣā is the only Masjid besides the Holy Ka'bah in Makkah which is mentioned by name in the Holy Qur'ān:

سُبْحَٰنَ ٱلَّذِىٓ أَسْرَىٰ بِعَبْدِهِۦ لَيْلًا مِّنَ ٱلْمَسْجِدِ ٱلْحَرَامِ إِلَى ٱلْمَسْجِدِ
ٱلْأَقْصَا ٱلَّذِى بَٰرَكْنَا حَوْلَهُۥ لِنُرِيَهُۥ مِنْ ءَايَٰتِنَآ ۚ إِنَّهُۥ هُوَ ٱلسَّمِيعُ ٱلْبَصِيرُ ۝١

Holy is He Who carried His servant by night from the Holy Masjid (in Makkah) to the farther Masjid (in Jerusalem) whose surroundings We have blessed that We might show him some of Our Signs. Indeed He alone is All-Hearing, All-Seeing.

[Al-Isrā' 17: 1]

This verse reports the miraculous journey of the Prophet Muḥammad ﷺ from Makkah to al-Aqṣā Sanctuary in al-Quds (Jerusalem) and thereafter through the seven heavens to the Sublime Throne. This was a literal journey undertaken by the Prophet Muḥammad ﷺ in body and in a state of wakefulness. This event binds al-Aqṣā Sanctuary and therefore the city of al-Quds (Jerusalem) within the tenets of Islamic belief.

To ignore al-Aqṣā Sanctuary would mean disassociating from this verse of the Qur'ān and therefore an individual would fall short of the Islamic requirement of total submission to the way of the Lord: "*O you who believe, submit into Islam wholeheartedly...*" (2: 208).

The fact that the Holy Prophet ﷺ regularly recited *Sūrah al-Isrā'* every night in ṣalāh emphasises not only the importance and virtue, but also the profundity of the message within the verse. This *sunnah* of the Prophet Muḥammad ﷺ is in great need of reviving:

'Ā'ishah ؓ reports that the Prophet ﷺ used to recite *Sūrah al-Isrā'* every night in his prayer.

[*Tirmidhī, Nasā'ī*]

2 A Blessed and Holy Land

THE "BLESSED LAND" under the Islamic ethos means land associated with *barakah* – the land over which Allah ﷻ has endowed spiritual and physical blessings from which all of humanity can derive benefit. The *barakah* also extends to the people who reside within this land, on condition that they conform to the commands of Allah ﷻ, i.e., practise Islam.

Al-Aqṣā Sanctuary has been honoured and glorified by Allah ﷻ and showered with His divine blessings for the benefit, enlightenment and guidance of all mankind.

The Qur'ān states that the blessings of this land are for "*al-'Ālamīn*" – which means for all the world's creatures until eternity. It implies that the blessings are not restricted to any specific group of people or species, rather encompassing all living and non-living things.

The boundaries of this "blessed land" are not clear and there are differences of opinion about its exact extent. Some classical Islamic scholars of the Qur'ān and aḥādīth, including Ibn Kathīr, al-Qurṭubī and Ibn al-Jawzī, consider the whole area of al-Shām (modern-day Lebanon, Syria, Jordan and Palestine) as blessed. Other interpreters believe that the blessed land is contiguous from the Ḥijāz (Saudi Arabia) through al-Shām to Egypt. A further, and maybe a more logical opinion, is that within the area of the modern Middle East, there are pockets of "blessed land" like the compound of al-Aqṣā Sanctuary, the Prophet's ﷺ Masjid in Madinah and the Holy Masjid in Makkah. However, in all the opinions on the extent of the "blessed land", al-Aqṣā Sanctuary is included.

The blessings of al-Aqṣā Sanctuary in particular and al-Shām area in general is expounded in the Holy Qur'ān and the traditions of the Prophet Muḥammad ﷺ:

THE QUR'ĀN

1. *Sūrah al-Isrā'* makes a direct reference to al-Aqṣā Sanctuary with no ambiguity and Allah ﷻ informs us that the Masjid al-Aqṣā and its surrounding area has been "blessed" by Him for mankind to reap spiritual and material benefit.

سُبْحَـٰنَ ٱلَّذِىٓ أَسْرَىٰ بِعَبْدِهِۦ لَيْلًا مِّنَ ٱلْمَسْجِدِ ٱلْحَرَامِ إِلَى ٱلْمَسْجِدِ
ٱلْأَقْصَا ٱلَّذِى بَـٰرَكْنَا حَوْلَهُۥ لِنُرِيَهُۥ مِنْ ءَايَـٰتِنَآ ۚ إِنَّهُۥ هُوَ ٱلسَّمِيعُ ٱلْبَصِيرُ ۝١

Holy is He Who carried His servant by night from the Holy Mosque (in Makkah) to the farther Mosque (in Jerusalem) whose surroundings We have blessed that We might show him some of Our Signs. Indeed He alone is All-Hearing, All-Seeing.

[Al-Isrā' 17: 1]

2. After Mūsā ﷺ took the Banū Isrā'īl away from the tyranny of the Pharaoh in Egypt to the outskirts of Palestine, he directed them to enter the "*Holy Land*". The Holy Land described in the Holy Qur'ān is the land of Palestine in general and the city of al-Quds more specifically.

يَٰقَوۡمِ ٱدۡخُلُواْ ٱلۡأَرۡضَ ٱلۡمُقَدَّسَةَ ٱلَّتِي كَتَبَ ٱللَّهُ لَكُمۡ وَلَا تَرۡتَدُّواْ عَلَىٰٓ
أَدۡبَارِكُمۡ فَتَنقَلِبُواْ خَٰسِرِينَ ٢١

My people! Enter the holy land which Allah has ordained for you; and do not turn back for then you will turn about losers.
[Al-Mā'idah 5: 21]

It is significant to note that the Qur'ān refers to the land of Palestine as "holy" and not as a "promised" land. A clear indication of the all-encompassing nature of Almighty Allah ﷻ – to bestow favours on the whole of mankind rather than a specific group. It cannot be befitting for the Creator of mankind to favour one group over any other by the simple virtue of their birth, rather those that are nearest to Him are those who are most pious – that is those who abide by His commands.

3. In *Sūrah al-A'rāf*, Allah ﷻ further informs us that He poured His Blessings on to the land both East and West of al-Quds (Jerusalem). This was the abode of Banū Isrā'īl at that time, and was most probably in the era of Prophet Sulaymān عليه السلام.

وَأَوۡرَثۡنَا ٱلۡقَوۡمَ ٱلَّذِينَ كَانُواْ يُسۡتَضۡعَفُونَ مَشَٰرِقَ ٱلۡأَرۡضِ وَمَغَٰرِبَهَا ٱلَّتِي
بَٰرَكۡنَا فِيهَاۖ وَتَمَّتۡ كَلِمَتُ رَبِّكَ ٱلۡحُسۡنَىٰ عَلَىٰ بَنِيٓ إِسۡرَٰٓءِيلَ بِمَا صَبَرُواْۖ
وَدَمَّرۡنَا مَا كَانَ يَصۡنَعُ فِرۡعَوۡنُ وَقَوۡمُهُۥ وَمَا كَانُواْ يَعۡرِشُونَ ١٣٧

And We made those who had been persecuted inherit the eastern and western lands which We had blessed. Thus your Lord's gracious promise was fulfilled to the Children of Israel, for they had endured with patience; and We destroyed all that Pharaoh and his people had wrought, and all that they had built.
[Al-A'rāf 7: 137]

The land of Palestine was under the rule of the Egyptian Pharaoh and hence the reference to the levelling to the ground of the great buildings which the Pharaoh erected.

4. Prophet Ibrāhīm عليه السلام and his immediate family were deported by his clansmen from the city of his birth, Ur, in a country called Sumer (modern-day Iraq), for preaching the *tawḥīd* of Allah سبحانه وتعالى. The Qur'ān informs us that Ibrāhīm عليه السلام was delivered by Allah سبحانه وتعالى to the land which Allah سبحانه وتعالى has "*blessed for the nations*". This land, which Allah سبحانه وتعالى eloquently refers to as "*blessed for the nations*", is the glorious land of Palestine. Prophet Ibrāhīm عليه السلام is believed to have re-constructed the Masjid al-Aqṣā in al-Quds (Jerusalem) with his son Isḥāq (Isaac) عليه السلام.

وَنَجَّيْنَـٰهُ وَلُوطًا إِلَى ٱلْأَرْضِ ٱلَّتِى بَـٰرَكْنَا فِيهَا لِلْعَـٰلَمِينَ ﴿٧١﴾

And We saved him and Lot and brought him to the land upon which We had bestowed Our blessings for all the people of the world.

[Al-Anbiyā' 21: 71]

5. The kingdom of Prophet Sulaymān عليه السلام was in present-day Palestine, with al-Quds (Jerusalem) as its capital. The Qur'ān refers to the whole area where Prophet Sulaymān عليه السلام travelled as *"the land which We had blessed"*.

وَلِسُلَيْمَـٰنَ ٱلرِّيحَ عَاصِفَةً تَجْرِى بِأَمْرِهِۦٓ إِلَى ٱلْأَرْضِ ٱلَّتِى بَـٰرَكْنَا فِيهَا ۚ
وَكُنَّا بِكُلِّ شَىْءٍ عَـٰلِمِينَ ﴿٨١﴾

And We subdued the strongly raging wind to Solomon which blew at his bidding towards the land We blessed. We know everything.

[Al-Anbiyā' 21: 81]

6. In *Sūrah Saba'* there is a reference to the people of Saba' in Yemen who frequented the Frankincense highway via Arabia to Syria in the north and Egypt to the west. The *"cities on which We had poured Our blessings"* refers to the cities of al-Shām including al-Quds (Jerusalem).

وَجَعَلْنَا بَيْنَهُمْ وَبَيْنَ ٱلْقُرَى ٱلَّتِي بَـٰرَكْنَا فِيهَا قُرًى ظَـٰهِرَةً وَقَدَّرْنَا فِيهَا ٱلسَّيْرَ ۖ سِيرُوا۟ فِيهَا لَيَالِىَ وَأَيَّامًا ءَامِنِينَ ﴿١٨﴾

We placed other prominent towns between them, the towns that We had blessed and had set well-measured stages between them. Move back and forth between them, night and day, in perfect security.

[Saba' 34: 18]

The verses of the Holy Qur'ān indicate that unlike any other place on earth, Allah ﷻ has blessed the land of Palestine. Allah ﷻ has blessed and honoured this area prior to any event or incident through His Great Mercy and the subsequent events that took place there are further reasons by which the followers built their love and affection for this area. No doubt the presence of Prophets and the historical link to them builds a bond but it is Allah ﷻ through His Great Mercy and Wisdom, who has chosen the area around al-Aqṣā Sanctuary to be blessed.

AḤĀDĪTH

The Prophet Muḥammad ﷺ is reported to have said, "Allah ﷻ has blessed what lies between al-Arish (in Egypt) and the Euphrates and has made Palestine particularly holy".

[*Kanz al-'Ummāl*]

Zayd ibn Thābit ﷺ reports that the Prophet ﷺ said, "How blessed is al-Shām! The Companions around asked: "Why is that?" The Messenger ﷺ replied, "I see the angels of Allah ﷻ spread their wings over al-Shām". Ibn 'Abbās ﷺ added, "and the Prophets lived in it. There is not a single inch in al-Quds (Jerusalem) where a Prophet has not prayed or an angel not stood".

[*Tirmidhī and Imām Aḥmad*]

'Abdullāh ibn 'Umar ﷺ reports that the Prophet ﷺ said, "O Allah! Bestow Your blessings on our Shām! O Allah! Bestow Your blessings on our Yemen". The people said, "And also on our Najd".[2] He said, "O Allah! Bestow Your blessings on our Shām! O Allah! Bestow Your blessings on our Yemen". The people said, "O Allah's Apostle! And also on our Najd". I think the third time the Prophet ﷺ said, "There (in Najd) is the place of earthquakes and afflictions and from there comes out the side of the head of Satan".

[*Ṣaḥīḥ al-Bukhārī*]

The Prophet Muḥammad ﷺ prayed for the blessing of the people of al-Shām. Anas ibn Mālik ﷺ reports that the Prophet ﷺ looked towards Iraq, al-Shām and Yemen then said, "O Allah! Bring their hearts over to Your obedience and relieve them of their burdens".

[*Tirmidhī*]

Once the Prophet ﷺ advised 'Abdullāh ibn Hawālah ﷺ to join the army in al-Shām, over any other. However, the Prophet ﷺ noticing Ibn Hawālah's indifference said, "Do you know what Allah says about al-Shām? Allah said, "Al-Shām you are the quintessence of My lands (*ṣafwatī min bilādī*) and I shall inhabit you with the chosen ones among My servants".

[*Al-Ṭabarānī*]

Shurayh ibn 'Ubayd said that the people of al-Shām were mentioned in front of 'Alī ibn Abī Ṭālib ﷺ while he was in Iraq and someone said to him, "Curse them, Commander of the Believers". He replied, "No. I heard the Prophet ﷺ say, 'The Substitutes (*al-Abdāl*) are in al-Shām – forty men – every time one of them dies, Allah replaces another in his place. By means of them Allah brings down the rain, gives us victory over our enemies and averts punishment from the people of al-Sham'".

[*Imām Aḥmad*]

3 The Place and Direction of Worship

A. MASJID AL-AQṢĀ: THE FIRST *QIBLAH*

Masjid al-Aqṣā was the first *qiblah* of Muslims (the direction Muslims face when performing daily prayers). Throughout the Prophet Muḥammad's ﷺ stay in Makkah, he turned his body towards al-Quds (Jerusalem) for prayers. The Prophet's biographers state that he used to stand towards the southern end of the Ka'bah so that while he was in prayer facing al-Quds (Jerusalem) the Ka'bah was in front of him.

The centrality of al-Aqṣā Sanctuary for Muslims is not only greatly emphasised by the fact that it was the first *qiblah* but also by the fact that all the prayers conducted by the previous generation facing Masjid al-Aqṣā remain valid. Further, the aḥādīth emphasising the respect of the first *qiblah*, Masjid al-Aqṣā, makes it incumbent upon Muslims to continue with the love, affection and reverence of al-Aqṣā Sanctuary.

The Qur'ān

Although al-Quds (Jerusalem) and Masjid al-Aqṣā are not mentioned by name in the verses below, the reference to the first *qiblah* in Islamic tradition is, beyond a shadow of doubt, none other than Masjid al-Aqṣā and the city of al-Quds (Jerusalem).

The Prophet ﷺ and the first generation Muslims prayed facing al-Quds (Jerusalem) throughout the Makkan era and for sixteen or seventeen months in Madinah until the verses below to change the *qiblah* were revealed.

۞ سَيَقُولُ ٱلسُّفَهَآءُ مِنَ ٱلنَّاسِ مَا وَلَّىٰهُمْ عَن قِبْلَتِهِمُ ٱلَّتِى كَانُوا۟ عَلَيْهَا ۚ قُل لِّلَّهِ
ٱلْمَشْرِقُ وَٱلْمَغْرِبُ ۚ يَهْدِى مَن يَشَآءُ إِلَىٰ صِرَٰطٍ مُّسْتَقِيمٍ ﴿١٤٢﴾ وَكَذَٰلِكَ
جَعَلْنَٰكُمْ أُمَّةً وَسَطًا لِّتَكُونُوا۟ شُهَدَآءَ عَلَى ٱلنَّاسِ وَيَكُونَ ٱلرَّسُولُ عَلَيْكُمْ
شَهِيدًا ۗ وَمَا جَعَلْنَا ٱلْقِبْلَةَ ٱلَّتِى كُنتَ عَلَيْهَآ إِلَّا لِنَعْلَمَ مَن يَتَّبِعُ ٱلرَّسُولَ مِمَّن
يَنقَلِبُ عَلَىٰ عَقِبَيْهِ ۚ وَإِن كَانَتْ لَكَبِيرَةً إِلَّا عَلَى ٱلَّذِينَ هَدَى ٱللَّهُ ۗ وَمَا
كَانَ ٱللَّهُ لِيُضِيعَ إِيمَٰنَكُمْ ۚ إِنَّ ٱللَّهَ بِٱلنَّاسِ لَرَءُوفٌ رَّحِيمٌ ﴿١٤٣﴾ قَدْ نَرَىٰ
تَقَلُّبَ وَجْهِكَ فِى ٱلسَّمَآءِ ۖ فَلَنُوَلِّيَنَّكَ قِبْلَةً تَرْضَىٰهَا ۚ فَوَلِّ وَجْهَكَ شَطْرَ
ٱلْمَسْجِدِ ٱلْحَرَامِ ۚ وَحَيْثُ مَا كُنتُمْ فَوَلُّوا۟ وُجُوهَكُمْ شَطْرَهُۥ ۗ وَإِنَّ ٱلَّذِينَ
أُوتُوا۟ ٱلْكِتَٰبَ لَيَعْلَمُونَ أَنَّهُ ٱلْحَقُّ مِن رَّبِّهِمْ ۗ وَمَا ٱللَّهُ بِغَٰفِلٍ عَمَّا
يَعْمَلُونَ ﴿١٤٤﴾ وَلَئِنْ أَتَيْتَ ٱلَّذِينَ أُوتُوا۟ ٱلْكِتَٰبَ بِكُلِّ ءَايَةٍ مَّا تَبِعُوا۟ قِبْلَتَكَ ۚ
وَمَآ أَنتَ بِتَابِعٍ قِبْلَتَهُمْ ۚ وَمَا بَعْضُهُم بِتَابِعٍ قِبْلَةَ بَعْضٍ ۚ وَلَئِنِ ٱتَّبَعْتَ أَهْوَآءَهُم مِّنۢ
بَعْدِ مَا جَآءَكَ مِنَ ٱلْعِلْمِ ۙ إِنَّكَ إِذًا لَّمِنَ ٱلظَّٰلِمِينَ ﴿١٤٥﴾ ٱلَّذِينَ ءَاتَيْنَٰهُمُ
ٱلْكِتَٰبَ يَعْرِفُونَهُۥ كَمَا يَعْرِفُونَ أَبْنَآءَهُمْ ۖ وَإِنَّ فَرِيقًا مِّنْهُمْ لَيَكْتُمُونَ
ٱلْحَقَّ وَهُمْ يَعْلَمُونَ ﴿١٤٦﴾ ٱلْحَقُّ مِن رَّبِّكَ ۖ فَلَا تَكُونَنَّ مِنَ ٱلْمُمْتَرِينَ ﴿١٤٧﴾ وَلِكُلٍّ
وِجْهَةٌ هُوَ مُوَلِّيهَا ۖ فَٱسْتَبِقُوا۟ ٱلْخَيْرَٰتِ ۚ أَيْنَ مَا تَكُونُوا۟ يَأْتِ بِكُمُ ٱللَّهُ جَمِيعًا ۚ

إِنَّ ٱللَّهَ عَلَىٰ كُلِّ شَيْءٍ قَدِيرٌ ﴿١٤٨﴾ وَمِنْ حَيْثُ خَرَجْتَ فَوَلِّ وَجْهَكَ شَطْرَ
ٱلْمَسْجِدِ ٱلْحَرَامِ ۖ وَإِنَّهُۥ لَلْحَقُّ مِن رَّبِّكَ ۗ وَمَا ٱللَّهُ بِغَٰفِلٍ عَمَّا تَعْمَلُونَ ﴿١٤٩﴾
وَمِنْ حَيْثُ خَرَجْتَ فَوَلِّ وَجْهَكَ شَطْرَ ٱلْمَسْجِدِ ٱلْحَرَامِ ۚ وَحَيْثُ مَا
كُنتُمْ فَوَلُّوا۟ وُجُوهَكُمْ شَطْرَهُۥ لِئَلَّا يَكُونَ لِلنَّاسِ عَلَيْكُمْ حُجَّةٌ إِلَّا ٱلَّذِينَ
ظَلَمُوا۟ مِنْهُمْ فَلَا تَخْشَوْهُمْ وَٱخْشَوْنِى وَلِأُتِمَّ نِعْمَتِى عَلَيْكُمْ وَلَعَلَّكُمْ
تَهْتَدُونَ ﴿١٥٠﴾

And it is thus that We appointed you to be the community of the middle way so that you might be witnesses to all mankind and the Messenger might be a witness to you. We appointed the direction which you formerly observed so that We might distinguish those who follow the Messenger from those who turn on their heels. For it was indeed burdensome except for those whom Allah guided. And Allah will never leave your faith to waste. Allah is full of gentleness and mercy to mankind.

We see you oft turning your face towards the sky; now We are turning you to the direction that will satisfy you. Turn your face towards the Holy Mosque, and wherever you are, turn your faces towards it in Prayer. Those who have been granted the Scripture certainly know that this (injunction to change the direction of Prayer) is right and is from their Lord. Allah is not heedless of what they do.

And yet no matter what proofs you bring before the People of the Book they will not follow your direction of Prayer; nor will you follow their direction of Prayer. None is prepared to follow the other's direction of Prayer. Were you to follow their desires in disregard of the knowledge which has come to you, you will surely be reckoned among the wrong-doers.

Those to whom We have given the Scripture recognize the place (towards which one must turn in Prayer) as fully as they recognize their own sons, this even though a group of them knowingly conceals the Truth. This is a definite Truth from your Lord; be not, then, among the doubters.

Everyone has a direction towards which he turns; so excel one another in good works. Allah will bring you all together wherever you might be, for nothing is beyond His power.

From wheresoever you might come forth turn your face towards the Holy Mosque; for that indeed is the Truth from your Lord, and Allah is not heedless of what you do.

From wheresoever you come forth turn your faces towards the Holy Mosque, and wheresoever you may be, turn your faces towards it in Prayer so that none may have an argument against you, unless they be those immersed in wrong-doing. Do not fear them, but fear only Me so that I may complete My favour upon you; perhaps you will be guided to the Right Way.

[Al-Baqarah 2: 143-150]

Aḥādīth

Al-Barā' ibn 'Āzib ❀ narrates, "When the Prophet ﷺ came to Madinah, he stayed first with his (grandfather's) maternal uncles from Anṣār. He offered his prayers facing Bayt al-Maqdis (Jerusalem) for sixteen or seventeen months, but he wished that he could pray facing the Ka'bah (in Makkah). The first prayer which he offered facing the Ka'bah was the 'Aṣr prayer in the company of some people. Then one of those who had offered that prayer with him came out and passed by some people in a Masjid who were bowing during their prayers (facing Jerusalem). He said addressing them, 'By

Allah, I testify that I have prayed with Allah's Apostle facing Makkah (the Ka'bah)'. Hearing that, those people changed their direction towards the Ka'bah immediately. The Jews and the people of the scriptures used to be pleased to see the Prophet ﷺ facing Jerusalem in prayers but when he changed his direction towards the Ka'bah, during the prayers, they disapproved of it".

[*Ṣaḥīḥ al-Bukhārī*]

Al-Barā' ؓ added, "Before we changed our direction towards the Ka'bah in prayers, some Muslims had died or had been killed and we did not know what to say about them (regarding their prayers). Allah ﷻ then revealed: *And Allah would never make your faith (prayers) to be lost (i.e. the prayers of those Muslims facing Bayt al-Maqdis were valid)* 2: 143".

[*Ṣaḥīḥ al-Bukhārī*]

'Abdullāh ibn 'Umar ؓ narrates, "We prayed with the Prophet ﷺ facing al-Quds (Jerusalem) for sixteen or seventeen months. Then Allah ﷻ ordered him to turn his face towards the *qiblah* (in Makkah)".

[*Ṣaḥīḥ al-Bukhārī*]

Anas ؓ, who lived the longest after the Prophet Muḥammad ﷺ passed away, narrates, "None remains of those who prayed facing both *qibla*s (Jerusalem and Makkah) except me".

[*Ṣaḥīḥ al-Bukhārī*]

The change of *qiblah* is one of the most important events that unified the Ummah and became the integrating force for Muslims all over the globe. It was also a natural change from the second house of Allah (Masjid al-Aqṣā) to the first (Ka'bah). However, the importance of the first *qiblah*, Jerusalem, remains true and holds a special historical and theological significance for Muslims.

Ibn Isḥāq, one of the classical biographers of the Prophet ﷺ, relates an interesting episode: While the Prophet ﷺ was still in Makkah some people from Madinah had accepted Islam and one of them was al-Barā' ibn Marūr رضي الله عنه. While on their way to Makkah, al-Barā' decided to pray facing the Ka'bah, for if he faced al-Aqṣā Sanctuary, he would have his back to the Ka'bah and Makkah, where the Prophet ﷺ resided. His companions instructed him to face al-Aqṣā Sanctuary as the Prophet ﷺ did, but his love for the Prophet ﷺ won over reason. When they arrived in Makkah they approached the Prophet ﷺ and reported about al-Barā's decision. The Prophet ﷺ said, "You would have had a *qiblah* if you had kept to it". Al-Barā' is reported to have returned to the first *qiblah* after this. It is the same al-Barā who stretched his hand out first to pledge allegiance with the Prophet ﷺ from the people of Madinah.

B. PLACE OF WORSHIP

Apart from being the first *qiblah,* Jerusalem has served many Prophets and has been honoured by their presence. Al-Aqṣā Sanctuary, in particular has been a place of meditation and retreat for many Prophets, including Ādam عليه السلام, Ibrāhīm عليه السلام, Isḥāq عليه السلام, Dāwūd عليه السلام, Sulaymān عليه السلام, Arāmiyah عليه السلام, Zakariyā عليه السلام, Yaḥyā عليه السلام and also Sayyidatunā Maryam, mother of 'Isā عليه السلام. The connection between these great Prophets with al-Aqṣā Sanctuary and the surrounding area further extols the virtues of al-Aqṣā Sanctuary. Muslims hold all the Prophets of Allah in reverence and make no distinctions between them; therefore all places affiliated with these great Prophets are strongly bound with the hearts of the Muslim people.

1. *Reference to Prophet* Dāwūd ﵇

۞ وَهَلْ أَتَىٰكَ نَبَؤُا۟ ٱلْخَصْمِ إِذْ تَسَوَّرُوا۟ ٱلْمِحْرَابَ ﴿٢١﴾ إِذْ دَخَلُوا۟ عَلَىٰ دَاوُۥدَ
فَفَزِعَ مِنْهُمْ ۖ قَالُوا۟ لَا تَخَفْ ۖ خَصْمَانِ بَغَىٰ بَعْضُنَا عَلَىٰ بَعْضٍ فَٱحْكُم بَيْنَنَا
بِٱلْحَقِّ وَلَا تُشْطِطْ وَٱهْدِنَآ إِلَىٰ سَوَآءِ ٱلصِّرَٰطِ ﴿٢٢﴾

Has the story of the litigants reached you – of those who entered his private chambers by climbing over the wall?
As they came upon David – and he was frightened of them – they said: "Be not afraid. We are just two litigants: one of us has committed excess against the other. So judge rightly between us, and be not unjust; and guide us to the Right Way."

[Ṣād 38: 21-22]

This event narrated in the Qur'ān relates to two individuals who surprised Dāwūd ﵇ by entering his *miḥrāb* (niche) while he was busy praising Allah ﷻ. This *miḥrāb*, referred to in the Qur'ān, was within the compound of al-Aqṣā Sanctuary. The *miḥrāb* of Dāwūd within al-Aqṣā Sanctuary is thought to have been destroyed during the earthquake of the Fatimid era.

2. *Reference to* Sayyidatunā Maryam

The mother of Sayyidatunā Maryam, Hannah, vowed to Allah ﷻ that if He were to give her a child she would offer it to His service. When Sayyidatunā Maryam was born, her mother was perturbed as she was expecting a boy and the tradition of the time demanded that a girl could not be placed in the service of Allah's house. However, she kept her vow and took Sayyidatunā Maryam to al-Quds (Jerusalem) and placed her in the custody of her uncle Zakariyā ﵇ who was married to Hannah's sister.

Sayyidatunā Maryam was placed in one of the *miḥrābs* (niches) adjoining Masjid al-Aqṣā where she meditated and prayed to the Lord. The fact that Sayyidatunā Maryam served in al-Aqṣā Sanctuary is an important historical fact, which should emphasise the importance of this blessed Sanctuary to the believers.

This verse refers to the miracle of how Allah سبحانه وتعالى provided for Sayyidatunā Maryam's sustenance with fruits that were out-of-season. It is generally accepted that where there is evidence of Allah's blessings and miracles descending in a particular place on earth, His favours flow more readily in this same place for the believers.

فَتَقَبَّلَهَا رَبُّهَا بِقَبُولٍ حَسَنٍ وَأَنۢبَتَهَا نَبَاتًا حَسَنًا وَكَفَّلَهَا زَكَرِيَّا ۖ كُلَّمَا دَخَلَ
عَلَيْهَا زَكَرِيَّا ٱلْمِحْرَابَ وَجَدَ عِندَهَا رِزْقًا ۖ قَالَ يَٰمَرْيَمُ أَنَّىٰ لَكِ هَٰذَا ۖ
قَالَتْ هُوَ مِنْ عِندِ ٱللَّهِ ۖ إِنَّ ٱللَّهَ يَرْزُقُ مَن يَشَآءُ بِغَيْرِ حِسَابٍ ﴿٣٧﴾

Thereupon her Lord graciously accepted Mary and vouchsafed to her a goodly growth and placed her in the care of Zechariah. Whenever Zechariah visited her in the sanctuary, he found her provided with food. He asked her: "Mary, how did this come to you?" She said: "It is from Allah. Allah provides sustenance to whom He wills beyond all reckoning."

[Āl 'Imrān 3: 37]

3. *Reference to Prophet* Zakariyā عليه السلام

Zakariyā عليه السلام not only meditated within al-Aqṣā Sanctuary but he was also the Imām of the Masjid al-Aqṣā. On one ocassion he visited Maryam, who was residing in a private *miḥrāb* attached to the Masjid. He was surprised to find fresh out-of-season fruits in her room. Upon enquiring where they were from, he was told by Maryam that the fruits were from Allah. After noticing Allah's favours upon Maryam, Zakariyā عليه السلام prayed to Allah for the blessings of a child. At this time, he was 90 years old and his wife was of a similar age. Despite this, his prayers in al-Aqṣā Sanctuary were accepted and Allah ﷻ favoured him with a son and named him Yaḥyā (John) عليه السلام.

فَنَادَتْهُ ٱلْمَلَٰٓئِكَةُ وَهُوَ قَآئِمٌ يُصَلِّى فِى ٱلْمِحْرَابِ أَنَّ ٱللَّهَ يُبَشِّرُكَ بِيَحْيَىٰ
مُصَدِّقًۢا بِكَلِمَةٍ مِّنَ ٱللَّهِ وَسَيِّدًا وَحَصُورًا وَنَبِيًّا مِّنَ ٱلصَّٰلِحِينَ ﴿٣٩﴾

> *As he stood praying in the sanctuary, the angels called out to him: "Allah gives you good tidings of John (Yaḥyā), who shall confirm a command of Allah, shall be outstanding among people, utterly chaste, and a Prophet from among the righteous."*
>
> [Āl 'Imrān 3: 39]

The area of al-Aqṣā Sanctuary is where Allah's ﷻ mercies have descended and His believers' supplication was accepted. It is also the hope of the faithful that their *du'ās* will also be readily accepted in such sanctuaries. As Zakariyā عليه السلام sought Allah's favours after observing the favours bestowed upon Sayyidatunā Maryam by Allah ﷻ, we are also guided to follow suit and seek Allah's favour on such places.

4. ***Honour of Allah's House***

The general analysis is to honour all houses where the worship of Allah ﷻ is conducted, but some commentators state that this refers to the three blessed Mosques of Makkah, Madinah and al-Quds (Jerusalem).

فِى بُيُوتٍ أَذِنَ ٱللَّهُ أَن تُرْفَعَ وَيُذْكَرَ فِيهَا ٱسْمُهُۥ يُسَبِّحُ
لَهُۥ فِيهَا بِٱلْغُدُوِّ وَٱلْءَاصَالِ ﴿٣٦﴾

(Those who are directed to this Light are found) in houses which Allah has allowed to be raised and wherein His name is to be remembered: in them people glorify Him in the morning and in the evening.

[Al-Nūr 24: 36]

وَمَنْ أَظْلَمُ مِمَّن مَّنَعَ مَسَٰجِدَ ٱللَّهِ أَن يُذْكَرَ فِيهَا ٱسْمُهُۥ وَسَعَىٰ فِى
خَرَابِهَآ ۚ أُو۟لَٰٓئِكَ مَا كَانَ لَهُمْ أَن يَدْخُلُوهَآ إِلَّا خَآئِفِينَ ۚ لَهُمْ فِى ٱلدُّنْيَا
خِزْىٌ وَلَهُمْ فِى ٱلْءَاخِرَةِ عَذَابٌ عَظِيمٌ ﴿١١٤﴾

Who is more iniquitous than he who bars Allah's places of worship, that His name be mentioned there, and seeks their destruction? It does not behove such people to enter them, and should they enter, they should enter in fear. There is degradation for them in this world and a mighty chastisement in the Next.

[Al-Baqarah 2: 114]

4 Through Symbolic Expression

THE PREVIOUS CHAPTERS outlined direct and indirect references made in the Holy Qur'ān regarding al-Quds (Jerusalem). The Holy Qur'ān, in its own eloquent and unique style, also refers to al-Quds through symbols.

وَٱلتِّينِ وَٱلزَّيْتُونِ ۝١ وَطُورِ سِينِينَ ۝٢ وَهَٰذَا ٱلْبَلَدِ ٱلْأَمِينِ ۝٣ لَقَدْ خَلَقْنَا ٱلْإِنسَٰنَ فِىٓ أَحْسَنِ تَقْوِيمٍ ۝٤ ثُمَّ رَدَدْنَٰهُ أَسْفَلَ سَٰفِلِينَ ۝٥

By the fig and the olive; and by the Mount Sinai, and by this city (of Makkah), a haven of peace: surely We created man in the best mould; then We reverted him to the lowest of the low.

[Al-Tīn 95: 1-5]

Besides the direct interpretation of this verse there are several scholars who interpret these verses in the symbolic sense. The main views are:

1. The fig and olive represent mountains, the Mount of Figs in Damascus and the Mount of Olives in al-Quds (Jerusalem) just outside the walls of al-Aqṣā Sanctuary. As for the secure city there is unanimity in it being Makkah.

2. The fig and olive refer to the Masjid of Damascus and al-Aqṣā in al-Quds (Jerusalem) respectively.
3. The fig and olive refer to two places, Damascus and al-Quds (Jerusalem); this would concur with the second being Mount Sinai and the third being Makkah.

The greatness and lofty standing of al-Aqṣā Sanctuary can be gauged by the fact that Allah ﷻ swears an oath by these cities as they represent the most blessed places on earth.

This verse of Allah's swearing by al-Quds (Jerusalem) and its surrounding area was revealed in Makkah before the Hijrah in 622.

5 Through Seasonal Expression

THE HOLY QUR'ĀN adopts various approaches to highlight an issue and it is no different for al-Quds where we now see al-Quds being referred to through seasonal expression.

لِإِيلَـٰفِ قُرَيْشٍ ۝١ إِۦلَـٰفِهِمْ رِحْلَةَ ٱلشِّتَآءِ وَٱلصَّيْفِ ۝٢

Since the Quraysh became accustomed, accustomed to the journey of winter and summer.

[Quraysh 106: 1-2]

The Quraysh were admired and honoured by the Arab nomads for being the custodians of the Ka'bah in Makkah. This provided an ideal opportunity for the Quraysh to travel in safety. As merchants, they capitalised on this and travelled towards al-Shām and al-Quds (Jerusalem) during the hot Arabian summer and towards Yemen during the winter.

The historical accounts of Quraysh visiting al-Shām and the Roman emperor's court are well substantiated.

This verse, therefore, refers to the summer journeys of Quraysh to al-Shām in general and al-Quds (Jerusalem) in particular, referring indirectly to al-Quds (Jerusalem) and al-Aqṣā Sanctuary.

6 Prophets and People

IF GREAT PERSONALITIES enrich a place, then al-Quds (Jerusalem) is second to none. The greatest Prophets have either lived in or passed by the blessed city of al-Quds (Jerusalem). Hence, the significance of al-Aqṣā Sanctuary and Palestine is further enhanced by both the presence of noble Prophets and major events that occurred during the lifetime of these great men.

A. Prophet Ibrāhīm ﵇

وَنَجَّيْنَـٰهُ وَلُوطًا إِلَى ٱلْأَرْضِ ٱلَّتِى بَـٰرَكْنَا فِيهَا لِلْعَـٰلَمِينَ ﴿٧١﴾

And We saved him and Lot and brought him to the land upon which We had bestowed Our blessings for all the people of the world.

[Al-Anbiyā' 21: 71]

Prophet Ibrāhīm ﵇ migrated from his hometown of Ur in modern-day Iraq with his wife Sārah and nephew Lūṭ ﵇ and moved towards Palestine and settled there. The particular city of Palestine in which he first settled is a matter of conjecture. However, after a short period, he and his wife Sārah moved towards Egypt where they encountered a tyrannical leader.

The Egyptian tyrant was enchanted by Sārah's beauty and tried to seduce her. However, she was protected from him by Allah ﷾ who debilitated his hand when he tried to touch her. The tyrant begged Sārah to "break the spell" because he thought she had bewitched him. Sārah prayed to Allah ﷾ and the tyrant was cured. Again, he tried to get hold of Sārah and a second time his hand became debilitated. He once again asked Sārah to "break the spell" and she prayed to Allah ﷾ and he was cured. The tyrant was now convinced that Sārah was a witch and he became scared of her. To safeguard himself from her, he offered gifts and a maid called Hājar, to escape further spells. Sārah and Ibrāhīm ﵇ returned to Palestine and settled there.

Prophet Ibrāhīm ﵇ later married Hājar. Although Ibrāhīm ﵇ was very old (some say 80 years) Hājar bore him a son. Thereafter, Ibrāhīm ﵇ was commanded by Allah ﷾ to take his wife Hājar and their young son, Ismāil ﵇, to the Arabian Desert (modern-day Makkah) and leave them there. He followed the command of Allah and left Hājar and Ismāil in Makkah and returned to Palestine. Throughout his lifetime, Ibrāhīm ﵇ made several visits to the growing settlement of Makkah to see his son Ismāil ﵇ and together they re-built the Ka'bah.

However, Sārah, who remained in Palestine, also became pregnant in her old age and a second son called Isḥāq ﵇ was born. The Holy Qur'ān states:

وَبَشَّرْنَٰهُ بِإِسْحَٰقَ نَبِيًّا مِّنَ ٱلصَّٰلِحِينَ ﴿١١٢﴾

And We gave him the good news of Isaac, a Prophet and among the righteous ones.

[Al-Ṣaffāt 37: 112]

This good news of the birth of Isḥāq ﵇ was given to Ibrāhīm ﵇ in Palestine when he was approximately 100 years old. Isḥāq ﵇

lived with his father in and around al-Quds (Jerusalem), where he preached, traded, and eventually grew old and died. The graves of Ibrāhīm عليه السلام and Isḥāq عليه السلام are very near al-Quds (Jerusalem) in the city of Khalīl now called Hebron.

Ibrāhīm عليه السلام re-built the Ka'bah in Makkah with his first son Ismāil عليه السلام, and the Masjid al-Aqṣā in al-Quds (Jerusalem) with his other son Isḥāq عليه السلام.

When Ibrāhīm عليه السلام arrived in Palestine, according to Genesis XIV:18-20, a person by the name of Melchizedek who is referred to as the king of Salem (thought to be where the name Jerusalem is derived from), offered Ibrāhīm عليه السلام a tithe (piece of land); however Ibrāhīm عليه السلام purchased this land from the king of Salem.

Again according to Genesis XIII:18, Ibrāhīm عليه السلام built on this land a *"tent"* to praise Allah سبحانه وتعالى and later Isḥāq عليه السلام re-built it. Isḥāq عليه السلام was the father of Ya'qūb عليه السلام, who in turn was the father of Yūsuf عليه السلام. When the children of Ya'qūb عليه السلام moved to Egypt, the "house of Allah" slipped out of view.

After Ādam عليه السلام, Ibrāhīm عليه السلام and Isḥāq عليه السلام, are the second group of Prophets who re-built Masjid al-Aqṣā.

B. Prophet Mūsā عليه السلام

The progeny of Yūsuf عليه السلام continued to live in Egypt until the coming of Mūsā عليه السلام, at which time the persecution of them was intensified. Under the guidance of Mūsā عليه السلام they escaped to the Holy Land – Palestine.

In all the verses below, the references to 'town' 'land' and 'place' refer to Palestine and the city of al-Quds (Jerusalem) in particular: *Enter this town* (2: 58), *enter the holy land* (5: 21), *O Mūsā! In this land are a people of exceeding strength* (5: 22), *Therefore will the land be out of their reach for forty years* (5: 26), *Dwell in this town and eat therein as you wish* (7: 161), *We settled the Children of Israel in a beautiful dwelling place* (10: 93), *Dwell securely in the land* (17: 104), *and to establish a firm place for them* (28: 6).

وَإِذْ قُلْنَا ٱدْخُلُوا۟ هَٰذِهِ ٱلْقَرْيَةَ فَكُلُوا۟ مِنْهَا حَيْثُ شِئْتُمْ رَغَدًا
وَٱدْخُلُوا۟ ٱلْبَابَ سُجَّدًا وَقُولُوا۟ حِطَّةٌ نَّغْفِرْ لَكُمْ خَطَٰيَٰكُمْ ۚ وَسَنَزِيدُ
ٱلْمُحْسِنِينَ ﴿٥٨﴾

And recall when We said: "Go into this town and eat abundantly of its food; but enter the gate a prostrate, saying, 'Repentance'. We will forgive you your sins and shall bestow more favour on the doers of good."

[Al-Baqarah 2: 58]

يَٰقَوْمِ ٱدْخُلُوا۟ ٱلْأَرْضَ ٱلْمُقَدَّسَةَ ٱلَّتِى كَتَبَ ٱللَّهُ لَكُمْ وَلَا تَرْتَدُّوا۟ عَلَىٰٓ
أَدْبَارِكُمْ فَتَنقَلِبُوا۟ خَٰسِرِينَ ﴿٢١﴾

My people! Enter the holy land which Allah has ordained for you; and do not turn back for then you will turn about losers.

[Al-Mā'idah 5: 21]

قَالُوا۟ يَٰمُوسَىٰٓ إِنَّ فِيهَا قَوْمًا جَبَّارِينَ وَإِنَّا لَن نَّدْخُلَهَا حَتَّىٰ يَخْرُجُوا۟ مِنْهَا
فَإِن يَخْرُجُوا۟ مِنْهَا فَإِنَّا دَٰخِلُونَ ﴿٢٢﴾

They answered: "Moses, therein live a ferocious people: we will not enter unless they depart from it; but if they do depart from it then we will surely enter it."

[Al-Mā'idah 5: 22]

قَالَ فَإِنَّهَا مُحَرَّمَةٌ عَلَيْهِمْ أَرْبَعِينَ سَنَةً يَتِيهُونَ فِى ٱلْأَرْضِ فَلَا تَأْسَ عَلَى
ٱلْقَوْمِ ٱلْفَٰسِقِينَ ﴿٢٦﴾

Allah said: "This land will now be forbidden to them for forty years and they will remain wandering about on the earth. Do not grieve over the condition of these transgressing people."

[Al-Mā'idah 5: 26]

وَإِذْ قِيلَ لَهُمُ ٱسْكُنُوا۟ هَٰذِهِ ٱلْقَرْيَةَ وَكُلُوا۟ مِنْهَا حَيْثُ شِئْتُمْ وَقُولُوا۟ حِطَّةٌ
وَٱدْخُلُوا۟ ٱلْبَابَ سُجَّدًا نَّغْفِرْ لَكُمْ خَطِيٓـَٰٔتِكُمْ سَنَزِيدُ ٱلْمُحْسِنِينَ ﴿١٦١﴾

And recall when it was said to them: "Dwell in this town and eat plentifully of whatever you please, and say: 'Repentance', and enter the gate prostrate. We shall forgive you your sins and shall bestow further favours on those who do good."

[Al-A'rāf 7: 161]

وَأَوْحَيْنَآ إِلَىٰ مُوسَىٰ وَأَخِيهِ أَن تَبَوَّءَا لِقَوْمِكُمَا بِمِصْرَ بُيُوتًا وَٱجْعَلُوا۟
بُيُوتَكُمْ قِبْلَةً وَأَقِيمُوا۟ ٱلصَّلَوٰةَ وَبَشِّرِ ٱلْمُؤْمِنِينَ ﴿٨٧﴾

And We directed Moses and his brother: "Prepare a few houses for your people in Egypt, and make your houses a direction for them to pray, and establish Prayer, and give glad tidings to the people of faith."

[Yūnus 10: 87]

وَلَقَدْ بَوَّأْنَا بَنِىٓ إِسْرَٰٓءِيلَ مُبَوَّأَ صِدْقٍ وَرَزَقْنَٰهُم مِّنَ ٱلطَّيِّبَٰتِ فَمَا ٱخْتَلَفُوا۟
حَتَّىٰ جَآءَهُمُ ٱلْعِلْمُ إِنَّ رَبَّكَ يَقْضِى بَيْنَهُمْ يَوْمَ ٱلْقِيَٰمَةِ فِيمَا
كَانُوا۟ فِيهِ يَخْتَلِفُونَ ﴿٩٣﴾

We settled the Children of Israel in a blessed land and provided them with all manner of good things. They only disagreed among themselves after knowledge (of the Truth had) come to them. Surely your Lord will judge among them on the Day of Resurrection concerning their disagreements.

[Yūnus 10: 93]

وَقُلْنَا مِنۢ بَعْدِهِۦ لِبَنِىٓ إِسْرَٰٓءِيلَ ٱسْكُنُوا۟ ٱلْأَرْضَ فَإِذَا جَآءَ وَعْدُ
ٱلْءَاخِرَةِ جِئْنَا بِكُمْ لَفِيفًا ١٠٤

And thereafter We said to the Children of Israel: "Now dwell in the land, but when the promised time of the Hereafter comes, We shall bring you all together."

[Al-Isrā' 17: 104]

وَنُمَكِّنَ لَهُمْ فِى ٱلْأَرْضِ وَنُرِىَ فِرْعَوْنَ وَهَٰمَٰنَ وَجُنُودَهُمَا
مِنْهُم مَّا كَانُوا۟ يَحْذَرُونَ ٦

And to grant them power in the land, and make Pharaoh and Hāmān and their hosts see what they had feared.

[Al-Qaṣaṣ 28: 6]

The biography of Mūsā عليه السلام is long; a brief summary should suffice: After Pharaoh began his persecution, Mūsā عليه السلام with his brother Hārūn (Aaron) عليه السلام guided the Banū Isrā'īl (Children of Israel) to flee from Egypt towards Palestine. After crossing the Red Sea, where Pharaoh and his men died, the Banū Isrā'īl began to argue and protest at the lack of water, food and shade. Mūsā عليه السلام prayed to Allah سبحانه وتعالى and all three were provided. Even after these favours their ungratefulness continued and they built a statue of a calf to worship in total contradiction to Mūsā's عليه السلام commands.

When they arrived on the outskirts of Palestine, Mūsā ﷺ commanded them to *enter the Holy Land* (5: 21), they nevertheless remonstrated, *O Mūsā! In this land are a people of exceeding strength: never shall we enter it until they leave it: if (once) they leave, then shall we enter* (5: 22).

Mūsā ﷺ assured them of victory if they marched forward and he also planned the attack for them – *Assault them at the (proper) gate, when you enter victory will be yours* (5: 23). However, the Banū Isrā'īl remained obstinate and said, *Mūsā, you and your Lord go and fight, we will wait here* (5: 24).

Mūsā ﷺ was deeply pained and felt dejected with the Banū Isrā'īl and thus he turned to Allah ﷻ, *O My Lord! I have power only over myself and my brother (Hārūn), so separate us from this rebellious people* (5: 25).

Allah ﷻ brought down His punishment on the ungrateful and recusant, *they shall be forbidden to enter the land for* 40 *years, while they wander about on earth and grieve not over the rebellious people* (5: 26).

The Banū Isrā'īl thus remained wandering aimlessly in the desert and it is narrated that only when all the adult members of the rebellious generation had died, did their descendants cross the River Jordan and move towards Jericho in Palestine. Even Mūsā ﷺ and his brother Hārūn ﷺ died before reaching the Holy Land. A ḥadīth *Qudsī* reports:

> Abū Hurayrah ؓ reports that the Prophet ﷺ said, "the angel of death was sent to Mūsā. When he came to Mūsā, Mūsā slapped him on the eye. The angel returned to Allah ﷻ and said, 'You have sent me to a servant who does not want to die'. Allah ﷻ ordered the angel, 'Return to him and tell him to put his hand on the back of an ox and for every hair that will come under it, he will be granted one year of life'. Mūsā said, 'O Lord! What will happen after that?' Allah ﷻ replied,

'Then death'. Mūsā decided, 'Let it be now'. Mūsā then requested Allah ﷻ to let him die close to the Sacred Land, so much so, that he would be at a distance of a stone's throw from it". Abū Hurayrah ؓ added, the Prophet ﷺ then said, "If I were there, I would show you his grave below the red sand hill on the side of the road".

[*Ṣaḥīḥ al-Bukhārī*]

C. Prophet Dāwūd ؑ

After the Banū Isrā'īl were delivered on the outskirts of the Holy Land by Mūsā ؑ, they came under the sway of the Philistines. After a few hundred years of living under the Philistines, they united behind Ṭalūt (Saul) who marched them forward to confront the Philistines. The Bible talks of the giant Goliath of the Philistines who challenged the Banū Isrā'īl to combat. However, it was not Saul who came out to confront Goliath but a young and unarmed Dāwūd ؑ. The well-known story of how Dāwūd ؑ brought the mighty Goliath down to his knees with only a sling, need not be retold here. *"And there went out a champion out of the camp of the Philistines, named Goliath, of Gath, whose height was six cubits and a span. And he had a helmet of brass upon his head, and he was armed with a coat of mail; and the weight of the coat was five thousand shekels of brass. And he had greaves of brass upon his legs and a target of brass between his shoulders. And the staff of his spear was like a weaver's beam..."* [1 Samuel XVII 4-7]

But Dāwūd was only armed with a sling and a few stones, "And Dāwūd put his hand in his bag and took out a stone and slung it, which smote the Philistine in his forehead, and he fell upon his face to the earth". [1 Samuel XVII 49]

Saul became the first King of the Israelites, but according to the Old Testament King Saul was jealous of Dāwūd ؑ and tried to get rid of him. Dāwūd ؑ retreated with his companions to the wilderness. They formed a coalition with their old enemies the Philistines and together attacked and killed Saul.

Dāwūd عليه السلام was crowned the Second King of the Israelites. Dāwūd عليه السلام, the King and Prophet, united his men and moved towards Jerusalem, which had been a Jebusite city since the 1800s BC. Dāwūd عليه السلام defeated the Jebusites and Jerusalem became his capital. Dāwūd عليه السلام integrated with the local population and did not kill nor expel the Jebusites. The Bible says, *"The Jebusites dwell with the children of Judea at Jerusalem unto this day"*. [Joshua XV 63]

Dāwūd عليه السلام spent almost his entire life in and around Palestine and, in particular, in the vicinity of al-Quds (Jerusalem). He served al-Aqṣā Sanctuary and many events in his noble life are focused around the Masjid al-Aqṣā.

إِنَّا سَخَّرْنَا ٱلْجِبَالَ مَعَهُۥ يُسَبِّحْنَ بِٱلْعَشِىِّ وَٱلْإِشْرَاقِ ﴿١٨﴾ وَٱلطَّيْرَ مَحْشُورَةً ۖ
كُلٌّ لَّهُۥٓ أَوَّابٌ ﴿١٩﴾ وَشَدَدْنَا مُلْكَهُۥ وَءَاتَيْنَٰهُ ٱلْحِكْمَةَ وَفَصْلَ
ٱلْخِطَابِ ﴿٢٠﴾

With him We had subjected the mountains that they join him in celebrating Allah's glory, evening and morning, and the birds, too, in their flocks, and turn again and again to celebrating Allah's glory. And We strengthened his kingdom and endowed him with wisdom and decisive judgement.

[Ṣād 38: 18-20]

۞ وَلَقَدْ ءَاتَيْنَا دَاوُۥدَ مِنَّا فَضْلًا ۖ يَٰجِبَالُ أَوِّبِى مَعَهُۥ وَٱلطَّيْرَ ۖ وَأَلَنَّا لَهُ ٱلْحَدِيدَ ﴿١٠﴾

We bestowed Our favour upon David. (We commanded): "O mountains, sing Allah's praises with him"; (and so did We command) the birds. We softened the iron for him.

[Saba' 34: 10]

Dāwūd عليه السلام was favoured with a melodious voice and the Qur'ān informs us that the hills and birds praised in unison the Greatness of the Lord, Allah ﷻ. These hills are none other than the hills of the city of al-Quds (Jerusalem). The Holy Qur'ān also refers to Dāwūd عليه السلام as the vicegerent; the only other Prophet referred to as vicegerent is Ādam عليه السلام. This could be because Dāwūd عليه السلام was not only a Prophet but also the king and ruler of Palestine.

يَـٰدَاوُۥدُ إِنَّا جَعَلْنَـٰكَ خَلِيفَةً فِى ٱلْأَرْضِ فَٱحْكُم بَيْنَ ٱلنَّاسِ
بِٱلْحَقِّ وَلَا تَتَّبِعِ ٱلْهَوَىٰ فَيُضِلَّكَ عَن سَبِيلِ ٱللَّهِ ۚ إِنَّ ٱلَّذِينَ يَضِلُّونَ عَن
سَبِيلِ ٱللَّهِ لَهُمْ عَذَابٌ شَدِيدٌۢ بِمَا نَسُوا۟ يَوْمَ ٱلْحِسَابِ ﴿٢٦﴾

(We said to him): "O David, We have appointed you vicegerent on earth. Therefore, rule among people and do not follow (your) desire lest it should lead you astray from Allah's Path. Allah's severe chastisement awaits those who stray away from Allah's Path, for they had forgotten the Day of Reckoning".

[Ṣād 38: 26]

Although for the Israelites the importance of al-Aqṣā Sanctuary (Mount Moriah) really begins with the era of Dāwūd عليه السلام, to Muslims Dāwūd عليه السلام forms a link in the chain that began with Ādam عليه السلام.

Dāwūd عليه السلام managed with great difficulty to unite the different Jewish tribes and also subdue other citizens. However, his total reign only lasted for around 40 years, from 1018 BC to 978 BC.

According to the Old Testament, Dāwūd عليه السلام was commanded by God to build an altar and Dāwūd عليه السلام complied by first purchasing land from Ornan [Arunah] the Jebusite (V18). Yet again the Bible points towards the righteousness of Dāwūd عليه السلام, of actually paying for land rather than usurping it on the pretext of it being “God Given”. Sulaymān عليه السلام finally completed the building of the Temple on this land (2 Chronicles III 1). The Holy Qur’ān states:

وَوَهَبْنَا لِدَاوُۥدَ سُلَيْمَـٰنَ ۚ نِعْمَ ٱلْعَبْدُ ۖ إِنَّهُۥٓ أَوَّابٌ ۝٣٠

We bestowed upon David (an illustrious son), Solomon. How excellent a servant (of Ours he was)! Indeed he constantly turned to Us in devotion.

[Ṣād 38: 30]

According to the Jewish tradition it is cited in the Aggadah that Dāwūd’s mother was a daughter of Ithra, an Ismailite. Dāwūd عليه السلام is also reported to have had three wives; Michal, daughter of King Saul; Maacah, daughter of the Canaanite King Talmal of Geshur; and Bathsheba, a Hittite from Giloh, who was the mother of Sulaymān عليه السلام.

It is extremely significant to emphasise the fact that the Bible states that Sulaymān’s mother was a Hittite. Under the Judaic law, the child’s religious line of heritage is from the mother and not the father. Therefore according to Judaic rule, Sulaymān عليه السلام is not a Jew and under the present-day Israeli Law, Sulaymān عليه السلام would not be allowed to reside in Palestine!

The story in the Old Testament accuses Dāwūd عليه السلام of adultery with Bathsheba, the mother of Sulaymān عليه السلام and conspiracy to murder Bathsheba’s husband Uriah, who was a general in Dāwūd’s army. *“And it came to pass in an evening that David arose from his bed and walked upon the roof of the house: and from there he saw a woman washing herself, and the woman was very beautiful.*

And David sent and enquired after the woman. And one said, It is Bathsheba, the daughter of Eliam, the wife of Uriah the Hittite.

And David sent for her and took her and she came unto him and he lay with her…

And the woman conceived, and sent and told David, and said, I am with child. [2 Samuel XI 2-5]

Thereafter, according to the Bible, Dāwūd conspired to get Uriah killed: *"send Uriah in the forefront of the hottest battle that he may be smitten and die".* [2 Samuel XI 15]

Islam states categorically that all of the Prophets were righteous men and free of sin. It is therefore incumbent upon Muslims to respect Dāwūd عليه السلام for his noble character and as a sinless Prophet of Allah ﷻ. For a Muslim to believe otherwise would expel him from the fold of Islam; such is the respect demanded of Muslims for the Prophets of Allah. The Qur'ān extols Dāwūd's عليه السلام character by calling him, "*...Our slave Dāwūd, endued with power. Verily, he ever turned in repentance to Allah"* (38: 17).

The Prophet Muḥammad ﷺ in *Ṣaḥīḥ al-Bukhārī*, is quoted as saying that Dāwūd عليه السلام was one of the noblest Prophets.

D. Prophet Sulaymān عليه السلام

After Dāwūd's death Sulaymān عليه السلام inherited his father's Kingdom. He resumed the construction of Masjid al-Aqṣā (Temple) which had been started during his father's era. Sulaymān عليه السلام ruled for a further 40 years, from 978 BC to 938 BC, thus making a total of 80 years rule between the two Prophets, Dāwūd عليه السلام and Sulaymān عليه السلام.

The following verses relate to Allah's favour upon Sulaymān عليه السلام by commanding the wind to be under Sulaymān's *"control"* in the land that Allah ﷻ says He has blessed. The blessed land in this verse of the Holy Qur'ān refers to Palestine. It was an honour for the land of Palestine that Sulaymān عليه السلام travelled through it with the aid of the wind, a miracle with which Allah had exclusively favoured Sulaymān عليه السلام. Palestine, a blessed land, was further exalted as it also became the place of Allah's special favours upon one of His Prophets.

وَلِسُلَيْمَـٰنَ ٱلرِّيحَ عَاصِفَةً تَجْرِى بِأَمْرِهِۦٓ إِلَى ٱلْأَرْضِ ٱلَّتِى بَـٰرَكْنَا فِيهَا ۚ
وَكُنَّا بِكُلِّ شَىْءٍ عَـٰلِمِينَ ﴿٨١﴾

And We subdued the strongly raging wind to Solomon which blew at his bidding towards the land We blessed. We know everything.

[Al-Anbiyā' 21: 81]

فَسَخَّرْنَا لَهُ ٱلرِّيحَ تَجْرِى بِأَمْرِهِۦ رُخَآءً حَيْثُ أَصَابَ ﴿٣٦﴾

We subjected the wind to him, so that it blew gently at his bidding, wherever he directed it.

[Ṣād 38: 36]

وَلِسُلَيْمَـٰنَ ٱلرِّيحَ غُدُوُّهَا شَهْرٌ وَرَوَاحُهَا شَهْرٌ ۖ وَأَسَلْنَا لَهُۥ عَيْنَ ٱلْقِطْرِ ۖ وَمِنَ
ٱلْجِنِّ مَن يَعْمَلُ بَيْنَ يَدَيْهِ بِإِذْنِ رَبِّهِۦ ۖ وَمَن يَزِغْ مِنْهُمْ عَنْ أَمْرِنَا نُذِقْهُ مِنْ
عَذَابِ ٱلسَّعِيرِ ﴿١٢﴾

And We subdued the wind to Solomon: its morning course was a month's journey and its evening course was a month's journey. We gave him a spring flowing with molten brass, and We subdued for him jinn who, by his Lord's permission, worked before him. Such of them as swerved from Our commandment, We let them taste the chastisement of the Blazing Fire.

[Saba' 34: 12]

وَلَقَدْ فَتَنَّا سُلَيْمَـٰنَ وَأَلْقَيْنَا عَلَىٰ كُرْسِيِّهِۦ جَسَدًا ثُمَّ أَنَابَ ﴿٣٤﴾

Surely We put Solomon to the test and cast upon his throne a mere body. Thereupon he penitently turned (to Us).

[Ṣād 38: 34]

قَالَ رَبِّ ٱغْفِرْ لِى وَهَبْ لِى مُلْكًا لَّا يَنۢبَغِى لِأَحَدٍ مِّنۢ بَعْدِىٓ ۖ إِنَّكَ أَنتَ ٱلْوَهَّابُ ﴿٣٥﴾

He said: "My Lord, forgive me and bestow upon me a kingdom such as none other after me will deserve. Surely You are the Bounteous Giver."

[Ṣād 38: 35]

وَلِسُلَيْمَـٰنَ ٱلرِّيحَ غُدُوُّهَا شَهْرٌ وَرَوَاحُهَا شَهْرٌ ۖ وَأَسَلْنَا لَهُۥ عَيْنَ ٱلْقِطْرِ ۖ وَمِنَ ٱلْجِنِّ مَن يَعْمَلُ بَيْنَ يَدَيْهِ بِإِذْنِ رَبِّهِۦ ۖ وَمَن يَزِغْ مِنْهُمْ عَنْ أَمْرِنَا نُذِقْهُ مِنْ عَذَابِ ٱلسَّعِيرِ ﴿١٢﴾ يَعْمَلُونَ لَهُۥ مَا يَشَآءُ مِن مَّحَـٰرِيبَ وَتَمَـٰثِيلَ وَجِفَانٍ كَٱلْجَوَابِ وَقُدُورٍ رَّاسِيَـٰتٍ ۚ ٱعْمَلُوٓا۟ ءَالَ دَاوُۥدَ شُكْرًا ۚ وَقَلِيلٌ مِّنْ عِبَادِىَ ٱلشَّكُورُ ﴿١٣﴾

And We subdued the wind to Solomon: its morning course was a month's journey and its evening course was a month's journey. We gave him a spring flowing with molten brass, and We subdued for him jinn who, by his Lord's permission, worked before him. Such of them as swerved from Our commandment, We let them taste the chastisement of the Blazing Fire. They made for him whatever he would desire: stately buildings, images, basins like water-troughs and huge, built-in cauldrons: "Work, O house of David, in thankfulness (to your Lord). Few of My servants are truly thankful."

[Saba' 34: 12-13]

Allah ﷻ even subjected the Jinn to Sulaymān's order, and he used the Jinn profitably and employed their energy towards building dams, large cauldrons *"Degs"* and whole cities. There is also an indication here that the Jinn were used in the re-construction of Masjid al-Aqṣā.

All the above verses of the Holy Qur'ān make a direct or an indirect reference to the land of Palestine, via events or people associated with the land of Palestine.

Upon Sulaymān's عليه السلام death, his son Rehoboam was crowned. However, within a very short period, a revolt began and hatred between the different Jewish tribes reared up and the kingdom was split in 922 BC. To the north, Israel was formed which later became known as Samaria. To the south, Judea was formed with Jerusalem as its capital.

A great rivalry ensued between these two neighbours and by 722 BC the Assyrians (from modern-day Syria) conquered and destroyed Israel.

Judea, where the children of Dāwūd عليه السلام lived, remained united and intact for a while. However, even here religious corruption crept in slowly, idolatry and superstition became the norm and even the Masjid al-Aqṣā (Temple) was not spared. "Altars and high places were erected on every hill and under every green tree. In Judea there were as many gods as there were towns. Images of gods in silver, wood and stone were erected in the houses. The Temple itself was once more desecrated by hideous idols".[3]

E. Prophet Arāmiyah (Jeremiah) عليه السلام

As the Jewish tribes slipped into spiritual corruption Prophet Arāmiyah (Jeremiah) عليه السلام was sent by Allah ﷻ to guide the people back onto the right path. He lived within al-Quds (Jerusalem) and warned the people of the pending punishment if they did not correct their ways. But the Jews did not listen or heed the advice of the Prophet, and instead locked him in a dungeon.

The Holy Qur'ān states:

وَقَضَيْنَآ إِلَىٰ بَنِىٓ إِسْرَٰٓءِيلَ فِى ٱلْكِتَـٰبِ لَتُفْسِدُنَّ فِى ٱلْأَرْضِ مَرَّتَيْنِ
وَلَتَعْلُنَّ عُلُوًّا كَبِيرًا ﴿٤﴾ فَإِذَا جَآءَ وَعْدُ أُولَىٰهُمَا بَعَثْنَا عَلَيْكُمْ عِبَادًا لَّنَآ أُو۟لِى
بَأْسٍ شَدِيدٍ فَجَاسُوا۟ خِلَـٰلَ ٱلدِّيَارِ ۚ وَكَانَ وَعْدًا مَّفْعُولًا ﴿٥﴾ ثُمَّ رَدَدْنَا
لَكُمُ ٱلْكَرَّةَ عَلَيْهِمْ وَأَمْدَدْنَـٰكُم بِأَمْوَٰلٍ وَبَنِينَ وَجَعَلْنَـٰكُمْ أَكْثَرَ
نَفِيرًا ﴿٦﴾ إِنْ أَحْسَنتُمْ أَحْسَنتُمْ لِأَنفُسِكُمْ ۖ وَإِنْ أَسَأْتُمْ فَلَهَا ۚ فَإِذَا جَآءَ وَعْدُ
ٱلْـَٔاخِرَةِ لِيَسُـۥٓـُٔوا۟ وُجُوهَكُمْ وَلِيَدْخُلُوا۟ ٱلْمَسْجِدَ كَمَا دَخَلُوهُ أَوَّلَ مَرَّةٍ
وَلِيُتَبِّرُوا۟ مَا عَلَوْا۟ تَتْبِيرًا ﴿٧﴾ عَسَىٰ رَبُّكُمْ أَن يَرْحَمَكُمْ ۚ وَإِنْ عُدتُّمْ عُدْنَا
وَجَعَلْنَا جَهَنَّمَ لِلْكَـٰفِرِينَ حَصِيرًا ﴿٨﴾

Then We clearly declared to the Children of Israel in the Book: "Twice you will make mischief in the land and will commit transgression." So, when the occasion for the first of the transgressions arrived, We raised against you some of Our creatures who were full of might, and they ran over the whole of your land. This was a promise that was bound to be fulfilled. Then We granted you an upper hand against them, and strengthened you with wealth and children, and multiplied your numbers. Whenever you did good, it was to your own advantage; and whenever you committed evil, it was to your own disadvantage. So, when the time of the fulfilment of the second promise arrived, (We raised other enemies that would) disfigure your faces and enter the Temple (of Jerusalem) as they had entered the first time, and destroy whatever they could lay their hands on. Your Lord may well show Mercy to you, but if you revert to your evil behaviour, We shall revert to chastising you. We have made Hell a prison for those who are thankless of Allah's bounties.

[Al-Isrā' 17: 4-8]

Allah ﷻ says in the Holy Qur'ān that He forewarned the Banū Isrā'īl in previous scriptures that they would create mischief twice and, on both occasions Allah ﷻ would send an enemy to destroy them. Many scholars are of the view that the two corruptions spoken of refer first, to the period of Arāmiyah عليه السلام in 586 BC and, second, to the Roman era when in 70 CE after the ascension of 'Īsā عليه السلام Jerusalem was destroyed.

Even in the present-day Torah the text of this first warning is to be found in the books of Yasayah, Yarmiyah, Hizqeel and Zakariyā.

As the Jews fell into transgression and rebellion against Allah's Command, as stated above, Prophet Arāmiyah عليه السلام was sent to guide them.

Around this time (6th Century BC), an empire was emerging in Babylon. In 586 Nebuchadnezzar, the King of Babylon, attacked Judea and destroyed it. Nebuchadnezzar eventually entered al-Quds (Jerusalem) and destroyed the Masjid al-Aqṣā (Temple) and imprisoned the Jewish population in chains, taking them all to Babylon. The Qur'ān informs us *"We raised against you some of Our creatures who were full of might, and they ran over the whole of your land. This was a promise that was bound to be fulfilled"*.

Ibn Kathīr, the great Islamic scholar, writes that while Nebuchadnezzar's army was looting and destroying the city they heard Jews crying "wish we had listened to Arāmiyah". Upon enquiry about him, the army learnt that Arāmiyah عليه السلام had predicted their victory in Judea. Arāmiyah عليه السلام was brought before Nebuchadnezzar, who was greatly impressed by him and offered him a high office. However, Arāmiyah عليه السلام declined, and the king released him.

After carrying away what they could, the Babylonians burnt down the city of al-Quds (Jerusalem). Thus, Judea ceased to exist as a nation.

The Holy Qur'ān alludes to this episode in verse 2:259. Imām al-Baghawī, in his *tafsīr* of the verse below states that "the hamlet" is most likely alluding to al-Quds (Jerusalem) and the person mentioned is most likely Prophet Arāmiyah عليه السلام.

أَوْ كَٱلَّذِى مَرَّ عَلَىٰ قَرْيَةٍ وَهِىَ خَاوِيَةٌ عَلَىٰ عُرُوشِهَا قَالَ أَنَّىٰ يُحْىِۦ هَٰذِهِ ٱللَّهُ بَعْدَ مَوْتِهَا ۖ فَأَمَاتَهُ ٱللَّهُ مِاْئَةَ عَامٍ ثُمَّ بَعَثَهُۥ ۖ قَالَ كَمْ لَبِثْتَ ۖ قَالَ لَبِثْتُ يَوْمًا أَوْ بَعْضَ يَوْمٍ ۖ قَالَ بَل لَّبِثْتَ مِاْئَةَ عَامٍ فَٱنظُرْ إِلَىٰ طَعَامِكَ وَشَرَابِكَ لَمْ يَتَسَنَّهْ ۖ وَٱنظُرْ إِلَىٰ حِمَارِكَ وَلِنَجْعَلَكَ ءَايَةً لِّلنَّاسِ ۖ وَٱنظُرْ إِلَى ٱلْعِظَامِ كَيْفَ نُنشِزُهَا ثُمَّ نَكْسُوهَا لَحْمًا ۚ فَلَمَّا تَبَيَّنَ لَهُۥ قَالَ أَعْلَمُ أَنَّ ٱللَّهَ عَلَىٰ كُلِّ شَىْءٍ قَدِيرٌ ﴿٢٥٩﴾

Or consider him by way of example who passed by a town that was fallen down upon its turrets. He exclaimed: "How will Allah restore life to this town that is now dead?" Allah then caused him to remain dead for a hundred years and then raised him to life, and asked him: "How long did you remain in this state?" He replied: "I remained so for a day or a part of a day." Allah rejoined: "No, you have rather stayed thus for a hundred years. But look at your food and your drink, there is no deterioration in them. And look at your ass (how its entire skeleton has rotted). And We did all this so that We might make you a token of instruction for people. And see how We will put the bones (of the ass) together and will clothe them with flesh." Thus when the reality became clear to him, he said: "I know that Allah has power over everything."

[Al-Baqarah 2: 259]

After a period had elapsed, Arāmiyah ﷺ returned to the city of al-Quds (Jerusalem) and found it desolate and destroyed. In despair, he wondered how Allah ﷻ would ever revive it. Allah ﷻ caused sleep to overtake him. When he awoke he was asked for how long had he been sleeping? He replied for part of a day, "No" was the reply. He was informed he had been sleeping for 100 years and, to show him Allah's Power, Allah ﷻ destroyed the stronger of the two, the donkey, reducing it to a skeleton, while the "weaker" food and drink remained intact and fine. Before his eyes, Allah ﷻ brought the donkey back to life and when Arāmiyah عليه السلام observed this miracle his despair for the destroyed city of al-Quds (Jerusalem) vanished, as he knew Allah ﷻ had Power over all things and, as promised, He would revive the city again.

Summary

The United Kingdom of Israel lasted for 96 years – from 1018 BC to 922 BC.

In 922 the kingdom was split in two:

- ISRAEL: The northern kingdom lasted for 200 years – 922 BC to 722 BC
- JUDEA: The southern kingdom lasted for 336 years – 922 BC to 586 BC

Around 600 BC, the Persian Empire, East of Babylon, was emerging under the leadership of Shah Cyrus. He attacked Babylon around 550 BC and occupied it and all other territories belonging to Babylon including the land of Canaan and Jerusalem.

The Persians were sympathetic to the Jews and allowed them the freedom to return to Jerusalem and rebuild their lives. Some did return but others chose to move to the more fertile and rich land of Persia. A new Persian King, Darius, was compassionate enough to not only allow the rebuilding of the Temple but also to aid the Jews financially and, thus, in around 538 BC the construction of the so-called second Jewish Temple began. Persian rule came to an end after 200 years in 330 BC when Alexander the Great occupied Jerusalem. This ushered in Greek culture, language and tradition to the area.

In the land of Canaan, Greek influence was no less and Jews as well as Canaanites buckled under its pressure. Greek colonies were established at Gaza and around the central plain of Palestine.

Hellenisation became so extreme that a statue of Jupiter was placed on the altar of the Temple (Masjid al-Aqṣā) and sacrifices were offered to it.

After several decades of assimilation to Greek culture, the Hasmonean Jews began what is known as the Maccabean revolt against the Seleucids. In 164 BC they captured Jerusalem but, immediately after the conquest, the Jews started fighting amongst themselves, as the ambitions of the different groups to be rulers became clear.

The Pharisees started a rebellion around 88 BC and captured Jerusalem from the Hasmoneans but could not hold onto power for long, as they lacked unity. Soon after, another Jewish sect of Pharisees tried to confront the Hasmoneans.

While the Jews were engaged in their internal rivalry a new Empire was emerging in Europe – the Romans – who conquered Jerusalem in 63 BC. The land of Palestine and all the other occupied territories were divided into Roman provinces and Rome appointed procurators as their servants to take charge of the day-to-day affairs. Rome demanded huge tax revenues from their procurators, who in turn, oppressed the general public and extorted great wealth for the Roman emperor.

The Romans appointed Herod over Jerusalem, a descendant of the Edomite tribe who had recently converted to Judaism. Herod, like the other Procurators, was for all intents and purposes a puppet of Rome from 37 to 4 BC.

During his governorship, Herod extended the Temple on a grand scale, but he angered the orthodox Jews by placing a Golden eagle at its entrance to please his Roman masters. Herod arrested the orthodox Jews, mainly the Pharisees, who removed the eagle in a rebellion, and had most of them executed.[4]

However, after Herod's death, his area of control was further divided among his three sons. This situation, however, did not last very long, as the whole of Palestine had become a Roman State after the year 44 CE.

F. Prophet 'Īsā ؏ and Sayyidatunā Maryam

In the midst of this mayhem, Allah ﷻ once more sent a Prophet to guide the Banū Isrā'īl onto the right path:

$$\text{إِذْ قَالَتِ ٱمْرَأَتُ عِمْرَٰنَ رَبِّ إِنِّى نَذَرْتُ لَكَ مَا فِى بَطْنِى مُحَرَّرًا فَتَقَبَّلْ مِنِّىٓ إِنَّكَ أَنتَ ٱلسَّمِيعُ ٱلْعَلِيمُ}$$

(He also heard) when 'Imrān's woman said: "O Lord! Behold, unto You do I vow that the child in my womb is to be devoted to Your exclusive service. Accept it, then, from me. Surely You alone are All-Hearing, All-Knowing."

[Āl 'Imrān 3: 35]

$$\text{فَلَمَّا وَضَعَتْهَا قَالَتْ رَبِّ إِنِّى وَضَعْتُهَآ أُنثَىٰ وَٱللَّهُ أَعْلَمُ بِمَا وَضَعَتْ وَلَيْسَ ٱلذَّكَرُ كَٱلْأُنثَىٰ وَإِنِّى سَمَّيْتُهَا مَرْيَمَ وَإِنِّىٓ أُعِيذُهَا بِكَ وَذُرِّيَّتَهَا مِنَ ٱلشَّيْطَٰنِ ٱلرَّجِيمِ}$$

But when she gave birth to a female child, she said: "O Lord! I have given birth to a female" – and Allah knew full well what she had given birth to – "and a male is not the same as a female. I have named her Mary and commit her and her offspring to You for protection from Satan, the accursed."

[Āl 'Imrān 3: 36]

These verses refer to Hannah, the mother of Sayyidatunā Maryam who vowed to place her child in the service of Masjid al-Aqṣā (Temple). However, when the child, Maryam, was born, Hannah was concerned as to how she would fulfil her promise, as girls were not allowed to serve or enter al-Aqṣā Sanctuary. Nevertheless, Zakariyā عليه السلام who at the time was the Imām of al-Aqṣā Sanctuary, built her a *miḥrāb* within the compounds of the al-Aqṣā Sanctuary where Sayyidatunā Maryam was able to stay and meditate.

وَإِذْ قَالَتِ ٱلْمَلَـٰٓئِكَةُ يَـٰمَرْيَمُ إِنَّ ٱللَّهَ ٱصْطَفَىٰكِ وَطَهَّرَكِ وَٱصْطَفَىٰكِ
عَلَىٰ نِسَآءِ ٱلْعَـٰلَمِينَ ﴿٤٢﴾

Then came the time when the angels said: "O Mary! Behold, Allah has chosen you, and has made you pure, and has exalted you above all the women in the world."

[Āl 'Imrān 3: 42]

وَٱذْكُرْ فِى ٱلْكِتَـٰبِ مَرْيَمَ إِذِ ٱنتَبَذَتْ مِنْ أَهْلِهَا مَكَانًا شَرْقِيًّا ﴿١٦﴾

(O Muḥammad), recite in the Book the account of Mary, when she withdrew from her people to a place towards the east.

[Maryam 19: 16]

۞ فَحَمَلَتْهُ فَٱنتَبَذَتْ بِهِۦ مَكَانًا قَصِيًّا ﴿٢٢﴾

Then she conceived him and withdrew with him to a far-off place.

[Maryam 19: 22]

فَأَجَآءَهَا ٱلْمَخَاضُ إِلَىٰ جِذْعِ ٱلنَّخْلَةِ قَالَتْ يَٰلَيْتَنِى مِتُّ قَبْلَ هَٰذَا
وَكُنتُ نَسْيًا مَّنسِيًّا ﴿٢٣﴾

And the pains of childbirth drove her to the trunk of a palm tree: she cried (in her anguish) "Ah! would that I had died before this! Would that I had been a thing forgotten and out of sight!"

[Maryam 19: 23]

إِذْ قَالَتِ ٱلْمَلَٰٓئِكَةُ يَٰمَرْيَمُ إِنَّ ٱللَّهَ يُبَشِّرُكِ بِكَلِمَةٍ مِّنْهُ ٱسْمُهُ ٱلْمَسِيحُ
عِيسَى ٱبْنُ مَرْيَمَ وَجِيهًا فِى ٱلدُّنْيَا وَٱلْءَاخِرَةِ وَمِنَ ٱلْمُقَرَّبِينَ ﴿٤٥﴾

And when the angels said: "O Mary! Allah gives you the glad tidings of a command from Him: his name shall be Messiah, Jesus, the son of Mary. He shall be highly honoured in this world and in the Next, and shall be one of those near stationed to Allah".

[Āl 'Imrān 3: 45]

وَيُكَلِّمُ ٱلنَّاسَ فِى ٱلْمَهْدِ وَكَهْلًا وَمِنَ ٱلصَّٰلِحِينَ ﴿٤٦﴾

And he shall speak to people in the cradle and also later when he grows to maturity and shall indeed be among the righteous."

[Āl 'Imrān 3: 46]

وَجَعَلْنَا ٱبْنَ مَرْيَمَ وَأُمَّهُۥٓ ءَايَةً وَءَاوَيْنَٰهُمَآ إِلَىٰ رَبْوَةٍ ذَاتِ قَرَارٍ وَمَعِينٍ ﴿٥٠﴾

And We made Mary's son, and his mother, a Sign, and We gave them refuge on a lofty ground, a peaceful site with springs flowing in it.

[Al-Mu'minūn 23: 50]

وَرَسُولًا إِلَىٰ بَنِىٓ إِسْرَٰٓءِيلَ أَنِّى قَدْ جِئْتُكُم بِـَٔايَةٍ مِّن رَّبِّكُمْ ۖ أَنِّىٓ أَخْلُقُ
لَكُم مِّنَ ٱلطِّينِ كَهَيْـَٔةِ ٱلطَّيْرِ فَأَنفُخُ فِيهِ فَيَكُونُ طَيْرًۢا بِإِذْنِ ٱللَّهِ ۖ وَأُبْرِئُ
ٱلْأَكْمَهَ وَٱلْأَبْرَصَ وَأُحْىِ ٱلْمَوْتَىٰ بِإِذْنِ ٱللَّهِ ۖ وَأُنَبِّئُكُم بِمَا
تَأْكُلُونَ وَمَا تَدَّخِرُونَ فِى بُيُوتِكُمْ ۚ إِنَّ فِى ذَٰلِكَ لَءَايَةً لَّكُمْ إِن
كُنتُم مُّؤْمِنِينَ ﴿٤٩﴾

And he will be a Messenger to the Children of Israel. (And when he came to them he said): "I have come to you with a Sign from your Lord. I will make for you from clay the likeness of a bird and then I will breathe into it and by the leave of Allah it will become a bird. I will also heal the blind and the leper, and by the leave of Allah I will bring the dead to life. I will also inform you of what things you eat and what you treasure up in your houses. Surely this is a Sign for you if you are true believers".

[Āl 'Imrān 3: 49]

إِذْ قَالَ ٱللَّهُ يَٰعِيسَىٰٓ إِنِّى مُتَوَفِّيكَ وَرَافِعُكَ إِلَىَّ وَمُطَهِّرُكَ مِنَ ٱلَّذِينَ كَفَرُوا۟
وَجَاعِلُ ٱلَّذِينَ ٱتَّبَعُوكَ فَوْقَ ٱلَّذِينَ كَفَرُوٓا۟ إِلَىٰ يَوْمِ ٱلْقِيَٰمَةِ ۖ ثُمَّ إِلَىَّ
مَرْجِعُكُمْ فَأَحْكُمُ بَيْنَكُمْ فِيمَا كُنتُمْ فِيهِ تَخْتَلِفُونَ ﴿٥٥﴾

(And it was part of His scheme) when Allah said, "O Jesus! I will recall you and raise you up to Me and will purify you (of the company) of those who disbelieve, and will set your followers above the unbelievers till the Day of Resurrection. Then to Me shall all of you return, and I shall judge between you regarding whatever you differed among yourselves".

[Āl 'Imrān 3: 55]

بَل رَّفَعَهُ ٱللَّهُ إِلَيۡهِۚ وَكَانَ ٱللَّهُ عَزِيزًا حَكِيمٗا ١٥٨

But Allah raised him to Himself. Allah is All-Mighty, All-Wise.
[Al-Nisā' 4: 158]

It is more than likely that it was near Jerusalem that Maryam's mother took a vow to place her child in the service of al-Aqṣā Sanctuary, and it was in al-Aqṣā Sanctuary that Sayyidatunā Maryam served and further received the tidings from Allah ﷻ about the miraculous birth of 'Īsā ﷺ.

Within the vicinity of Jerusalem (in Bethlehem) 'Īsā ﷺ was born and it is in and around Jerusalem that 'Īsā ﷺ preached to the Banū Isrā'īl. Finally, it is from Jerusalem that 'Īsā ﷺ was raised to his Lord. All these verses and incidents reinforce the importance of Palestine to Muslims.

As 'Īsā ﷺ grew older, he began to teach and command people to believe in one God and that there is no mediation between the Lord and His creation. This annoyed the Jews and as 'Īsā's popularity grew they became concerned about their status in society. The Jews began to plot and plan against 'Īsā ﷺ.

The Jewish high priest at the time was Caiaphas who called a meeting of leading Jews for a strategy to get rid of 'Īsā ﷺ.

According to the Bible, while the Jews were in a meeting, one of the twelve apostles of 'Īsā ﷺ, Judas Iscariot, came to them and offered, *"What will you give me if I deliver him ['Īsā] to you?"* Judas bargained with them until they agreed to give him thirty pieces of silver known as Shekels. The plot was thus laid for the capture of 'Īsā ﷺ.

However, only the Roman governor, at the time, Pontius Pilate, could decree the death penalty. Hence, the Jews went to Pilate and conspired against 'Īsā ﷺ with false and malicious claims and demanded that he be killed.

The Gospel of St Matthew states: *"Pilate said unto them, what shall I do with Jesus which is called Christ? They all say unto him, let him be crucified. And the Governor said, why, what evil has he done? But they cried out the more, saying, let him be crucified. When Pilate saw that he could prevail nothing, but that rather a tumult was made, he took water and washed his hands before the multitude, saying I am innocent of the blood of this just person: see you to it. They replied let his blood be on us and our children".*

It is further reported in the Bible that on one occasion as 'Īsā walked out of Jerusalem he prophesied the destruction of the Temple: *"And Jesus went out and departed from the Temple, and his disciples came to him for to show him the buildings of the Temple. And Jesus said unto them See you all these things? Verily I say unto you, there shall not be left here one stone upon another, that shall not be thrown down"* (Matthew XXIV 2).

In May 66 AD a revolt broke out throughout Palestine against the Romans, which resulted in many Romans and their collaborators, who were mainly Jewish Priests, being put to death.[5]

Rome dispatched an army headed by General Titus. Titus, the Roman General, quashed the revolt and in his wake flattened the whole city of Jerusalem, including Herod's Temple. The few Jews that remained were deported from Palestine and banned from even entering Jerusalem. This is the second of Allah's promises referred to in verse 17: 7-8, *"So when the second promise came to pass, [We raised up against you a people] that they may disgrace your faces and may enter the Mosque as they entered it the first time and that they may destroy, whatever they conquered with utter destruction. It may be that your Lord will have mercy upon you but if you return We shall return and We have made Hell a prison for the unbelievers".*

This brought an end to the Jewish presence in Palestine and for nearly the next 600 years, no Jew resided within the Blessed city of Jerusalem.

G. Christian Palestine

After the ascension of 'Īsā ﷺ, his teachings continued to spread amongst the poor. Christianity became established as a religion for the followers of 'Īsā ﷺ 32 years after his death. The Romans started to view Christianity as a threat and it was banned. The followers of Christianity were persecuted throughout the empire and their numbers began to dwindle. But in a turn of fortune, around 320 CE, the Roman emperor Constantine embraced Christianity and this single event not only saved Christianity but also helped spread it far and wide as it became the official religion of the empire.

After nearly 600 years of Roman rule over Jerusalem, the Persians occupied the city in 614 for a short period. Theophanes, the Roman historian, records the occupation: "In this year the Persians took Jordan, Palestine and its holy city in battle. At the hands of the Jews they killed many people in it. Some say 90,000.[6] The Jews, according to their means bought the Christians and then killed them. The Persians captured and led off to Persia Zacharia, the patriarch of Jerusalem, the precious life-giving wood (the supposed fragment of the "True Cross" on which Christ was crucified) and many prisoners. As a gesture of goodwill and a token of appreciation for assisting the Persians gain Jerusalem, the Jews were given administrative power in Jerusalem. This time, the Jews are alleged to have avenged their mistreatment by banishing all the Christians out of the city. Whatever was not destroyed during the invasion of Jerusalem by the Persians, the Jews made sure they razed it to the ground; even the Church of the Resurrection was not spared. But the Jewish administration did not last long as the Persians quickly became aware and concerned at the excessive oppression of the Christians. The Persians decided to hand the city back to the Christians. Under the leadership of Modestus, most of the Churches and Holy sites began to be renovated.

However within 8 years, in 622, Heraclius defeated the Persians and re-occupied Jerusalem. Yet again the Jews were banished from the Holy City by Heraclius. He expelled them, ordering that they should not be allowed to come within three miles of the Holy City. According to Butler, the adversity of exile from Jerusalem for the Jews was minimal compared to the edict that followed instructing the provinces throughout the empire to persecute them – "something like a general massacre of the Jews followed".[7]

H. The Ṣaḥābah

The Ṣaḥābah, or Companions of the Prophet Muḥammad ﷺ, recognised the holy status and the blessings of the land of Palestine in general and of Jerusalem in particular. Many of them travelled to the Holy City to visit the sacred places and pray there. Some of them travelled there in order to begin the rites of their pilgrimage (Ḥajj or 'Umrah) from the blessed land. Those that are known to have adorned their iḥrām from al-Aqṣā Sanctuary include: 'Umar ibn al-Khaṭṭāb ﷺ, the second righteous Caliph, Sa'd ibn Abī Waqqāṣ ﷺ, 'Abdullāh ibn 'Umar ﷺ, Tamīm al-Dārī ﷺ, 'Amr ibn al-'Āṣ ﷺ, Abū Hurayrah ﷺ, and 'Abdullāh ibn 'Abbās ﷺ.

Other Companions who are known to have visited Masjid al-Aqṣā include: 'Abdullāh ibn Salām ﷺ, 'Abd al-Raḥmān ibn 'Awf ﷺ, Abū Dardā' ﷺ, Abū Dharr al-Gaffārī ﷺ, Abū Mas'ūd al-'Anṣārī ﷺ, Abū 'Ubaydaḥ ibn al-Jarrāḥ ﷺ, 'Alqamah ﷺ, 'Awf ibn Mālik ﷺ, Bilāl ibn Rabāḥ ﷺ, Ḥabīb ibn Siba ﷺ, Jund ibn Junādah ﷺ, Ka'b al-Aḥbār ﷺ, Khālid ibn Sa'īd ﷺ, Khālid ibn Walīd ﷺ, Mas'ūd ibn Aws ﷺ, Mu'ādh ibn Jabal ﷺ, Mu'āwiyah ibn Abī Sufyān ﷺ, Salmān al-Fārisī ﷺ, 'Uqbah ibn 'Āmir ﷺ and Yazīd ibn Abī Sufyān ﷺ.

Many more of the Companions travelled to al-Quds (Jerusalem) to be honoured by witnessing the conclusion of the peace treaty. The Prophet's *muezzin* Bilāl ibn Rabāḥ ﷺ, who refused to raise the *adhān* after the Prophet's death, was one of the first persons to raise the *adhān* in al-Aqṣā Sanctuary after it was conquered. Moreover, many of the Companions died and are buried in the area; their graves are still recognised and visited by Muslims. They include: Shaddād ibn Aws ﷺ, Tamīm al-Dārī ﷺ and ʻUbādah ibn al-Ṣāmit ﷺ.

The ḥadīth below by Ya'lā ibn Shaddād ibn Aws ﷺ shows that the Masjid al-Aqṣā was a favoured and well-frequented place by the Companions, he reports:

> "I came to Mu'āwiyah in al-Quds (Jerusalem), he led us in Friday prayer. I saw that most of the people in the Masjid were the Companions of the Prophet ﷺ..."
>
> [*Sunan Abū Dāwūd*]

The tradition of the great Ṣaḥābah and our pious predecessors was to frequent al-Aqṣā Sanctuary to not only fulfil the Sunnah but also gain great reward for it. They further used al-Aqṣā Sanctuary as a centre of learning and meditation.

I. The Land of Scholars

Many scholars of Islam were born and lived in this blessed land including:

Imām al-Shāfi'ī – Born in Gaza
Ibn Ḥajar al-'Asqalānī – Lived in 'Asqalān
Ibn Qudāmah al-Maqdisī – Lived in Nablus
Mūsā ibn Nuṣayr, the conqueror of Spain – Lived in Hebron

Many thousands of pious people and scholars migrated and settled in the Holy City. Moreover, numerous followers and great scholars visited and stayed for short periods in al-Quds (Jerusalem). These include: Imām al-Ghazālī, al-Ḥasan al-Zuhrī, Bishr al-Ḥāfī and Dhū'l-Nūn al-Miṣrī. The famous Islamic scholar Imām al-Ghazālī used to teach in al-Aqṣā Sanctuary; it is reported that he wrote part of his famous treatise *Iḥyā' 'Ulūm al-Dīn* (The Revival of Religious Sciences) within al-Aqṣā Sanctuary.

Thus, the Islamic features of al-Quds (Jerusalem) have developed since the earliest times. Besides the Companions and scholars, Muslim Caliphs under Umayyad, 'Abbasid, Mamluk and Ottoman rule paid great attention to the Holy City in the fields of architecture, religion and the different branches of science.

J. The Martyrs

The soil of this blessed land has been mixed with the sacred blood of countless martyrs. Many decisive battles took place in Palestine where thousands of Muslims sacrificed themselves in the defence of al-Ḥaram al-Sharīf (al-Aqṣā Sanctuary) and for the sake of Allah ﷻ.

The European Crusaders slaughtered more than 70,000 Muslim civilians within the sanctuary of al-Aqṣā and the bodies of the martyrs where piled knee high. The streets of al-Quds (Jerusalem) became rivers of human blood. Thousands of Muslims were martyred in order to regain al-Aqṣā Sanctuary from the Crusaders especially in the battles of Ḥiṭṭīn where Ṣalāḥ al-Dīn al-Ayyūbī defeated the Crusaders, at the battle of 'Ayn Jālūt near al-Nāsirah where the Tartars were defeated, and in Acre and Caesarea where the last Crusader stronghold was captured.

Since 1948, over one hundred thousand Muslims have been martyred in Palestine due to the never-ending Israeli aggression against Palestinians. The modern-day Palestinians have been targetted as they form the barrier to the Jewish fundamentalist plan of occupying al-Quds (Jerusalem) and the Palestinians have become the protectors of al-Ḥaram al-Sharīf (al-Aqṣā Sanctuary) for the Ummah.

7 Through Events

A. Al-Isrā' and al-Mi'rāj

One of the most miraculous episodes in the life of the Prophet Muḥammad ﷺ was his remarkable journey (al-Isrā') from the Ka'bah in Makkah to al-Aqṣā Sanctuary in al-Quds (Jerusalem), followed by the ascension (al-Mi'rāj) to the sublime Throne of Almighty Allah ﷻ.

This journey probably took place one year before the Hijrah. The Prophet ﷺ ascended to the heavens in body and while he ﷺ was in a state of wakefulness.

سُبْحَـٰنَ ٱلَّذِىٓ أَسْرَىٰ بِعَبْدِهِۦ لَيْلًا مِّنَ ٱلْمَسْجِدِ ٱلْحَرَامِ إِلَى ٱلْمَسْجِدِ
ٱلْأَقْصَا ٱلَّذِى بَـٰرَكْنَا حَوْلَهُۥ لِنُرِيَهُۥ مِنْ ءَايَـٰتِنَآ إِنَّهُۥ هُوَ ٱلسَّمِيعُ ٱلْبَصِيرُ ﴿١﴾

Holy is He Who carried His servant by night from the Holy Masjid (in Makkah) to the farther Masjid (in Jerusalem) whose surroundings We have blessed that We might show him some of Our Signs. Indeed He alone is All-Hearing, All-Seeing.

[Al-Isrā' 17: 1]

Al-Isrā' cannot be underestimated for bringing to the fore the centrality of al-Aqṣā Sanctuary to the Muslims. It imbibed within the Muslim mind, the eternal heritage and link to al-Aqṣā Sanctuary that makes al-Quds (Jerusalem) one of the greatest symbols of Islam. It must be acknowledged that from all the places on earth, Allah ﷻ chose al-Aqṣā Sanctuary, thereby sanctifying it.

The incidents listed below, which took place during this incredible journey, further elevate a believer's love and devotion for al-Aqṣā Sanctuary and the city of Bayt al-Maqdis (Jerusalem):

[i] While the Prophet Muḥammad ﷺ was resting in the precincts of the Ka'bah, he was approached by angel Jibrā'īl and was asked to mount a celestial animal named al-Burāq. This steed took the Prophet ﷺ to al-Quds (Jerusalem) accompanied by Jibrā'īl, where they tied it to the Western wall. This part of the wall thus became known to Muslims as al-Burāq wall (Jews refer to it as the Wailing Wall).

[ii] The Prophet ﷺ was then led into the precincts of al-Ḥaram al-Sharīf (al-Aqṣā Sanctuary) and someone called the *adhān* (call to prayer) and the multitude of people who were assembled straightened their rows in anticipation of someone to lead the ṣalāh (prayer). Jibrā'īl took hold of the Prophet Muḥammad's ﷺ hand and led him to the front, on the *Muṣallah* (prayer mat) to lead the prayers. This made the Prophet Muḥammad ﷺ one of the first Imāms of Masjid al-Aqṣā in this Ummah.

[iii] When the prayers had finished Jibrā'īl asked the Prophet Muḥammad ﷺ if he knew who were behind him in prayer? He replied, "No". Jibrā'īl informed him that all the Messengers, whom Allah ﷻ had sent to earth, from Prophet Ādam عليه السلام to 'Īsā عليه السلام, had performed ṣalāh behind him. As it is the belief of Muslims that Allah ﷻ has sent thousands (some say around 120,000) of Messengers and they all

performed ṣalāh within al-Ḥaram al-Sharīf (al-Aqṣā Sanctuary), therefore every centimetre of this sanctuary is to be considered as blessed and honourable; the forehead of every noble Prophet has touched some ground of al-Aqṣā Sanctuary.

[iv] Al-Ḥaram al-Sharīf (al-Aqṣā Sanctuary) is the only known site on earth where all the Prophets performed ṣalāh together at one given time, led by the Prophet Muḥammad ﷺ.

[v] This incident also shows that Islam is an inclusive religion, bringing all the Prophets together and not segregating them or differentiating between them.

[vi] It is also in al-Aqṣā Sanctuary that the Prophet ﷺ was offered a glass of milk and a glass of wine and he chose the milk upon which Jibrā'īl said, "You have chosen *Fiṭrah* – if you had taken the wine your followers would have gone astray". 'Allamah Qurtubī reports, "When it was said concerning milk 'this is the *Fiṭrah*' it meant the nature on which your life is based. This explains the natural affinity between the pure nature of Islam and the first food of a baby and this is why the word *Fiṭrah* is used to symbolise the religion of Islam".

[vii] When the Prophet ﷺ reported the next morning to the Makkans that he had been to Bayt al-Maqdis (Jerusalem) and to the higher heavens during the night, the *Mushrikīn* (polytheists) began to laugh with glee because they believed they now had proof for calling the Prophet ﷺ a liar and one suffering from delusions. They first ran towards Abū Bakr ؓ, one of the closest Companions of the Prophet ﷺ and in a mocking gesture started saying, "What do you have to say about your friend who claims to have gone to Bayt al-Maqdis (Jerusalem) and returned in one night?" Abū Bakr ؓ with great sagacity replied, "If he

(Muḥammad) has said so, then he has indeed been there". This incredible answer dumbfounded the *Mushrikīn*. Abū Bakr ﷺ clarified it by saying, "I believe in things far more astounding, I believe that whatever revelations come to him are from the heavens". The *Mushrikīn,* like others today, could not get around to believing the truth and they rushed back to the Prophet Muḥammad ﷺ and began to quiz him about his journey. The ḥadīth states, "I had never before been as uneasy as I was at the time they interrogated me. Though I had seen Bayt al-Maqdis (Jerusalem) in al-Isrā', I could not recollect in detail the exact description. However, Allah ﷻ revealed before my very eyes an image of Bayt al-Maqdis (Jerusalem) and thereafter I was immediately able to answer the questions the Quraysh of Makkah asked me" (*Ṣaḥīḥ Muslim*).

[viii] An important historical fact is that when al-Isrā' and al-Mi'rāj took place, there were no complete buildings within al-Aqṣā Sanctuary; the only building present was the surrounding wall and maybe a few ruins. As the ḥadīth verifies that the Prophet ﷺ described the city of Bayt al-Maqdis (Jerusalem) and not any buildings within al-Aqṣā Sanctuary, this validates the Prophet Muḥammad's ﷺ claim of al-Isrā' and the authenticity of his Prophethood.

[ix] Furthermore, the verse in the Holy Qur'ān *"... to al-Aqṣā Masjid (in Jerusalem), whose precincts We did bless ..."* emphasises that the sacredness is associated with the place and not with any of the buildings. This is further verified by many aḥādīth. This fact is of extreme importance to note for the Muslims, as they should base their love, devotion and dedication in preserving the Islamic identity of the land and not just to a building within al-Ḥaram al-Sharīf (al-Aqṣā Sanctuary) or the city of Bayt al-Maqdis (Jerusalem).

[x] The fact that Allah ﷻ chose to make al-Aqṣā Sanctuary a station in this miraculous journey is noteworthy and it must be recalled that the Prophet Muḥammad ﷺ not only stopped at al-Aqṣā on his journey from Makkah to the Sublime Throne, but he also stopped there on the return journey.

[xi] In this incredible event of performing ṣalāh in al-Aqṣā Sanctuary, ʿĪsā ﷷ was amongst the Prophets. According to classical scholars, as ʿĪsā ﷷ was raised alive (and has not "died"), he is also honoured with the title of a Ṣaḥābī – a believer who saw the Prophet Muḥammad ﷺ.

[xii] The fact that the Prophet Muḥammad ﷺ led the prayers in al-Ḥaram al-Sharīf (al-Aqṣā Sanctuary) is a clear indication of him being the leader of all the Prophets.

There are numerous aḥādīth regarding al-Isrā' and al-Miʿrāj which have been narrated through approximately 25 Ṣaḥābah, to quote a few:

Abū Hurayrah ؓ narrates that the Prophet ﷺ said, "On the night Allah's Apostle was taken on a night journey (al-Isrā' al-Miʿrāj) two cups, one containing wine and the other milk, were presented to him at al-Quds (Jerusalem). He looked at them and took the cup of milk. Jibrā'īl said, "Praise be to Allah ﷻ who guided you to *al-Fiṭrah* (the right path); if you had taken (the cup of) wine, your nation would have gone astray".

[*Ṣaḥīḥ al-Bukhārī*]

Ibn ʿAbbās ؓ regarding the statement of Allah ﷻ in the Holy Qur'ān *"And that We have made the vision which We have shown you (as an actual eye witness) and the tree accursed in the Qur'ān, to be only a trial for the people"*. (al-Isrā' 17: 60). Ibn ʿAbbās

added: The sights which Allah's Apostle was shown on the Night Journey when he was taken to Bayt al-Maqdis (i.e. Jerusalem) were actual sights, (not dreams). And the Cursed Tree (mentioned) in the Qur'ān is the tree of Zaqqūm (itself).
[*Ṣaḥīḥ al-Bukhārī*]

Jābir ibn 'Abdullāh ﵁ relates that the Prophet ﷺ said, "When the people of Quraysh did not believe me (i.e. the story of my Night Journey), I stood up in al-Ḥijr and Allah ﷾ displayed Bayt al-Maqdis (Jerusalem) in front of me, and I began describing it to them while I was looking at it".
[*Ṣaḥīḥ al-Bukhārī*]

B. Calamities on the Jews

These events have been discussed earlier under Prophet Arāmiyah ﵇. It is important to note that in order to release Prophet Arāmiyah ﵇, Allah ﷾ used the Babylonians, non-believing fire worshippers. Allah ﷾ has no need for those who claim to worship Him but do not fulfil their duties. The responsibility of safeguarding al-Aqṣā Sanctuary is upon the whole Ummah, and not any particular group of people or leaders. The fate of al-Aqṣā Sanctuary will be as Allah ﷾ wills, but our individual duty is what matters in the analysis of our success or failure, as we will be brought to task on the Day of Judgement for our individual roles in this affair.

وَقَضَيْنَآ إِلَىٰ بَنِىٓ إِسْرَٰٓءِيلَ فِى ٱلْكِتَٰبِ لَتُفْسِدُنَّ فِى ٱلْأَرْضِ مَرَّتَيْنِ
وَلَتَعْلُنَّ عُلُوًّا كَبِيرًا ﴿٤﴾ فَإِذَا جَآءَ وَعْدُ أُولَىٰهُمَا بَعَثْنَا عَلَيْكُمْ عِبَادًا لَّنَآ أُو۟لِى
بَأْسٍ شَدِيدٍ فَجَاسُوا۟ خِلَٰلَ ٱلدِّيَارِ ۚ وَكَانَ وَعْدًا مَّفْعُولًا ﴿٥﴾ ثُمَّ رَدَدْنَا
لَكُمُ ٱلْكَرَّةَ عَلَيْهِمْ وَأَمْدَدْنَٰكُم بِأَمْوَٰلٍ وَبَنِينَ وَجَعَلْنَٰكُمْ أَكْثَرَ

نَفِيرًا ﴿٦﴾ إِنْ أَحْسَنتُمْ أَحْسَنتُمْ لِأَنفُسِكُمْ ۖ وَإِنْ أَسَأْتُمْ فَلَهَا ۚ فَإِذَا جَآءَ وَعْدُ
ٱلْءَاخِرَةِ لِيَسُـۥٓـُٔوا۟ وُجُوهَكُمْ وَلِيَدْخُلُوا۟ ٱلْمَسْجِدَ كَمَا دَخَلُوهُ أَوَّلَ مَرَّةٍ
وَلِيُتَبِّرُوا۟ مَا عَلَوْا۟ تَتْبِيرًا ﴿٧﴾ عَسَىٰ رَبُّكُمْ أَن يَرْحَمَكُمْ ۚ وَإِنْ عُدتُّمْ عُدْنَا ۘ
وَجَعَلْنَا جَهَنَّمَ لِلْكَـٰفِرِينَ حَصِيرًا ﴿٨﴾

Then We clearly declared to the Children of Israel in the Book: "Twice you will make mischief in the land and will commit transgression." So, when the occasion for the first of the transgressions arrived, We raised against you some of Our creatures who were full of might, and they ran over the whole of your land. This was a promise that was bound to be fulfilled. Then We granted you an upper hand against them, and strengthened you with wealth and children, and multiplied your numbers. Whenever you did good, it was to your own advantage; and whenever you committed evil, it was to your own disadvantage. So, when the time of the fulfilment of the second promise arrived, (We raised other enemies that would) disfigure your faces and enter the Temple (of Jerusalem) as they had entered the first time, and destroy whatever they could lay their hands on. Your Lord may well show Mercy to you, but if you revert to your evil behaviour, We shall revert to chastising you. We have made Hell a prison for those who are thankless of Allah's bounties..

[Al-Isrā' 17: 4-8]

أَوْ كَٱلَّذِى مَرَّ عَلَىٰ قَرْيَةٍ وَهِىَ خَاوِيَةٌ عَلَىٰ عُرُوشِهَا قَالَ أَنَّىٰ يُحْىِۦ
هَـٰذِهِ ٱللَّهُ بَعْدَ مَوْتِهَا ۖ فَأَمَاتَهُ ٱللَّهُ مِا۟ئَةَ عَامٍ ثُمَّ بَعَثَهُۥ ۖ قَالَ كَمْ لَبِثْتَ ۖ
قَالَ لَبِثْتُ يَوْمًا أَوْ بَعْضَ يَوْمٍ ۖ قَالَ بَل لَّبِثْتَ مِا۟ئَةَ عَامٍ فَٱنظُرْ إِلَىٰ

طَعَامِكَ وَشَرَابِكَ لَمْ يَتَسَنَّهْ ۖ وَٱنظُرْ إِلَىٰ حِمَارِكَ وَلِنَجْعَلَكَ
ءَايَةً لِّلنَّاسِ ۖ وَٱنظُرْ إِلَى ٱلْعِظَامِ كَيْفَ نُنشِزُهَا ثُمَّ نَكْسُوهَا لَحْمًا ۚ فَلَمَّا
تَبَيَّنَ لَهُۥ قَالَ أَعْلَمُ أَنَّ ٱللَّهَ عَلَىٰ كُلِّ شَىْءٍ قَدِيرٌ ﴿٢٥٩﴾

Or consider him by way of example who passed by a town that was fallen down upon its turrets. He exclaimed: "How will Allah restore life to this town that is now dead?" Allah then caused him to remain dead for a hundred years and then raised him to life, and asked him: "How long did you remain in this state?" He replied: "I remained so for a day or a part of a day." Allah rejoined: "No, you have rather stayed thus for a hundred years. But look at your food and your drink, there is no deterioration in them. And look at your ass (how its entire skeleton has rotted). And We did all this so that We might make you a token of instruction for people. And see how We will put the bones (of the ass) together and will clothe them with flesh." Thus when the reality became clear to him, he said: "I know that Allah has power over everything."

[Al-Baqarah 2: 259]

C. Heraclius' victory over the Persians

The incredible collapse of the Roman Empire 8 years before the Hijrah at the hands of the Persians was greatly celebrated by the pagan Makkans and became a further reason for jibes at the Muslims. Most of the Makkans allied themselves with the Persians, as they shared pagan beliefs and were against the Romans, who were Christians and close to the young Muslim group that had emerged in their home town. However, as the Makkans were celebrating the Persian victory, Allah ﷻ revealed the verse in which the Persian collapse was predicted. This gave solace to the young

Muslim community who were calling for the belief in one God and considered themselves close to the Christians.

$$\text{الٓمٓ ۝ غُلِبَتِ ٱلرُّومُ ۝ فِىٓ أَدْنَى ٱلْأَرْضِ وَهُم مِّنۢ بَعْدِ غَلَبِهِمْ سَيَغْلِبُونَ ۝}$$

Alif. Lām. Mīm. The Romans have been defeated in the neighbouring land; but after their defeat they shall gain victory in a few years.

[Al-Rūm 30: 1-3]

As discussed earlier, the Persians defeated the Romans and occupied Jerusalem in 614. However, as the Qur'ān had predicted, the Roman Emperor Heraclius gathered the Romans and defeated the Persians, re-occupying Jerusalem in 622. This verse, which foretold the Roman victory, was revealed in Makkah at the time of the Persian victory. The reference *"In a land close by"* refers to the area of al-Shām where the battle took place and this verse should be seen as a direct reference through events. When the verse was revealed around 6 or 7 years before the Hijrah (615), the pagan Makkans mocked the Muslim claim. The Persian forces appeared superior and no contemporary observer of the time could envisage the return of the destroyed Romans.

The Makkan pagans challenged Abū Bakr ؓ on the validity of this verse thereby undermining the call to the faith of Islam, which resulted in Abū Bakr ؓ claiming that within five years they would see the Romans win or he would give them 100 camels.

When the Prophet ﷺ learnt about this he asked Abū Bakr ؓ to say within 10 years as the Qur'anic word *"Biḍ'"* means a period from three to nine years and his challenge was amended accordingly.

As history bears testimony, Heraclius defeated the Persian Empire in 622, a period of less than 9 years. This prophecy of the Holy Qur'ān became a means for many people to accept Islam.

D. End of Time (Eschatological) Events

The area of al-Shām plays a central role in Islamic eschatology, with many, but not all, events being focused in the region. From the appearance of al-Dajjāl (the Anti-Christ); the presence of Imām al-Mehdī in al-Shām; the return of 'Īsā ﵇; to the killing of al-Dajjāl by 'Īsā ﵇ in Ludd; the Yajūj and Majūj (Gog and Magog); land sliding at three places – east, west and on the Arabian Peninsula; and the trumpet blast to end this world. Thus al-Shām and the blessed land of al-Quds gains importance from historical events and future events.

وَٱسْتَمِعْ يَوْمَ يُنَادِ ٱلْمُنَادِ مِن مَّكَانٍ قَرِيبٍ ﴿٤١﴾

Hearken on the Day when the caller will call from a place quite near.

[Qāf 50: 41]

"The Day" refers to the Day of Resurrection when the angel Isrāfīl will blow his trumpet bringing to an end our world and thereafter all the souls will arise to assemble for Judgement day to begin. There are scholars who have said *"a place quite near"* refers to al-Quds (Jerusalem). However, this can be considered an ambiguous reference, since a general consensus has not been reached and there exist many other plausible interpretations of this verse. In the absence of a direct reference to al-Quds (Jerusalem) we must suspend our judgement to the reference of *"a place quite near"*.

However, the aḥādīth indicate that major events towards the end of time will take place around al-Aqṣā Sanctuary:

Al-Nawwās ibn Sam'ān ﵁ narrates that the Prophet ﷺ said, "Before the Hour, 'Īsā ﵇ will descend upon a white mināret towards the east of Damascus in Syria, during the dawn prayer. The Muslim Imām will move from his place and request

'Īsā ﷺ to lead the prayer but he will refuse and pray behind the Imām, declaring himself as a member of the nation of the Prophet Muḥammad ﷺ".

[*Ṣaḥīḥ Muslim*]

Al-Nawwās ibn Samʿān al-Kalbī ؓ narrates that the Prophet ﷺ said, "If al-Dajjāl comes forth while I am amongst you then I shall challenge him on your behalf, but if he comes after I am not with you, a man must dispute on his own behalf, and Allah ﷻ will take to protect every Muslim. Those of you who live up to his time should recite over him the opening verses of *Sūrah Kahf*, for they are your protection from his trial". We asked, How long will he remain on the earth? He replied, "Forty days, one like a year, one like a month, one like a week and the rest of his days like yours". We asked, Will one day's prayer suffice us in this day which will be like a year? He replied, "No, you must make an estimate of its extent. Then 'Īsā, son of Maryam will descend at the white mināret to the east of Damascus. He will then confront al-Dajjāl at the gates of Ludd and kill him".

[*Sunan Abū Dāwūd*]

Mujamma ibn al-Ḥārith ؓ narrates that the Prophet ﷺ said, "Ibn Maryam ('Īsā ﷺ) will kill al-Dajjāl (Anti-Christ) at the door of Ludd (a town in Palestine)".[8]

[*Imām Aḥmad and Tirmidhī*]

Al-Nawwās ibn Samʿān ؓ narrates that the Prophet ﷺ said, "Al-Dajjāl (Anti-Christ) will appear on the way between Syria and Iraq and will spread mischief right and left".

[*Ṣaḥīḥ Muslim*]

The Messenger of Allah ﷺ said regarding al-Dajjāl: "He will stay in the land forty days; he will enter every place on earth except the Ka'bah, the Prophet's Masjid, al-Aqṣā Sanctuary, and Mount Sinai".

[*Imām Aḥmad*]

The events described, that will take place at the end of time around al-Shām, include a battle between the Muslims and non-believers, with the Muslims being led by Imām al-Mehdī. While this war is in progress, al-Dajjāl will make an appearance. Al-Dajjāl will be recognised by those who have faith, as they will be able to decipher three letters in Arabic inscribed on his forehead, which would read "Kāfir" (non-believer). Al-Dajjāl will finally lay claim to being the Messiah upon which the non-belivers and those weak in faith will begin to follow him.

While the world is in this oppression and tumult 'Īsā عليه السلام will descend to earth with the aid of two angels. At that time the Muslims will have assembled for the dawn prayer and will be about to begin the prayers. 'Īsā's عليه السلام descent will be "*upon a white minaret towards the east of Damascus*". Noticing this, the Muslims assembled for prayer, will first help 'Īsā عليه السلام down from the minăret like any human and 'Īsā عليه السلام will be asked to lead the prayers. He will decline and pray behind the Imām as a follower of the Prophet Muḥammad ﷺ. Thereafter 'Īsā عليه السلام will assume leadership of the Muslims and go after al-Dajjāl.

Al-Dajjāl will be aware of his imminent doom and his power will begin to wither. 'Īsā عليه السلام will confront and kill him at a place called Ludd, possibly the same town in present-day Occupied Palestine called Ludd.

After this, the Ya'jūj and Ma'jūj will appear and run riot throughout the earth, razing everything in their path. 'Īsā عليه السلام will retreat to the mountain of aṭ-Ṭur with the faithful. Thereafter, Allah will "rain down" a type of worm which will attach to the necks of Ya'jūj and Ma'jūj and kill them all.

Thereafter, all enmity will end and peace and security will prevail throughout the world. There will be no other religion except Islam and the world will become a peaceful and just place.

Muʿādh ibn Jabal ؓ reports that the Prophet ﷺ said, "The flourishing state of al-Quds (Jerusalem) will be when Yathrib (Madinah) is in ruins, the ruined state of Yathrib will be when the Great War comes, the outbreak of the Great War will be at the conquest of Constantinople and the conquest of Constantinople will be when al-Dajjāl (Anti-Christ) comes forth". He (the Prophet ﷺ) struck his thigh or his shoulder with his hand and said, "This is as true as you are here or as you are sitting (meaning Muʿādh ibn Jabal)".

[*Sunan Abū Dāwūd*]

Maymūnah bint Saʿd ؓ reports that she asked the Prophet ﷺ, "O Messenger of Allah, give us a pronouncement about al-Quds (Jerusalem)". The Prophet ﷺ replied, "It is the land where they will be raised (al-Ḥashr) and gathered (al-Maḥshar)".

[*Imām Aḥmad and al-Ṭabarānī*]

Muʿāwiyah ibn Haydah ؓ reports that the Prophet ﷺ motioned towards al-Shām with his hand and said, "You will be gathered there; some walking, some riding, some crawling on their faces".

[*Tirmidhī*]

Abū Hurayrah ؓ reports that the Prophet ﷺ said, "The hour will not come until the Muslims fight the Jews and defeat them. When a Jew hides behind a rock or a tree, it will say, O Muslim, O Slave of Allah! There is a Jew behind me, come and kill him! All the trees will do this except the box-thorn (al-gharqad) tree".

[*Imām Aḥmad and Ṣaḥīḥ Muslim*]

'Abdullāh ibn 'Amr ibn al-'Āṣ reports that the Prophet ﷺ said, "A time will come (meaning during the End of Time) when people will see no believer remaining on earth except that they would have gone to al-Shām".

[*Al-Dhahabī and al-Ḥākim*]

'Awf ibn Mālik reports that the Prophet ﷺ said, "The world will be destroyed forty years before al-Shām is".

[*Ibn 'Asākir*]

8 A Place of Migration

The virtues of al-Ḥaram al-Sharīf (al-Aqṣā Sanctuary) and its surrounding land are clear from the frequent references made to it in the Holy Qur'ān and aḥādīth. The aḥādīth re-emphasize the centrality of al-Aqṣā Sanctuary and expound many practical suggestions through which one can remain attached to this great and Holy site. The Prophet Muḥammad ﷺ made a great effort to extol the virtues of al-Aqṣā Sanctuary through various means to ensure that al-Aqṣā Sanctuary and its surrounding areas remain in the consciousness of the believers.

In most cases migration is only considered for economic, educational or political benefits. Although migration during the time of the Prophet Muḥammad ﷺ ended after the liberation of Makkah, those that move to al-Shām in general and Palestine in particular, for the sake of Allah, are considered to be the best of the earth's inhabitants.

This single narration of the Prophet Muḥammad ﷺ relating to Palestine is sufficient for every Muslim to become concerned, involved and strive towards ensuring that justice is established. If our own weakness prevents us from migrating to al-Shām or legislation prohibits us, then the least we can do in our country of domicile is to champion the cause of al-Ḥaram al-Sharīf (al-Aqṣā Sanctuary), or at least send assistance to the brothers and sisters in Palestine.

'Abdullāh ibn 'Umar ❀ reports that the Prophet ❀ said, "There will be migration upon migration. The best of the inhabitants of the earth will reside where Prophet Ibrāhīm ❀ migrated".

[*Sunan Abū Dāwūd*]

Umāmah al-Bāhilī ❀ reports that the Prophet ❀ said, "A group of my community will remain on truth, they will vanquish their enemy and those who disagree with them will not be able to harm them until Allah ❀ commands". "Where are these people?" the Companions asked. The Prophet ❀ replied, "In and around al-Quds (Jerusalem)".

[*Imām Aḥmad*]

'Abdullāh ibn Hawālah reports that the Prophet ❀ said, "At some point you will be [split into] standing armies: one army in al-Shām, one in Yemen and one in Iraq". 'Abd Allah ibn Hawālah asked the Prophet ❀, "Choose for me, Messenger of Allah in case I live to see that day". The Prophet ❀ replied, "You must go to al-Shām, for it is the chosen land of Allah in all His earth. He protects, by sending them there, the chosen ones among His servants. If you do not wish to go there, then go to Yemen. Allah has given me a guarantee concerning al-Shām and its people".

(Abū Idrīs al-Khawlānī would add after narrating the above ḥadīth, "And whoever has Allah as his guarantor shall never suffer loss".)

[*Sunan Abū Dāwūd and Imām Aḥmad*]

The fourth pious Caliph, 'Alī ❀ stated: "Glad tidings for the residents of Bayt al-Maqdis when trials appear. The one who remains there will be considered a fighter in the way of Allah. A time will come upon the people when one of them will say, "I wish I were a blade of straw between the bricks of Bayt al-Maqdis".

'Abd al-Raḥman ibn Yazīd al-Azdī al-Dārānī asked the *Tābi'ī* Abū Sallām Mamṭūr al-Ḥabashī, "What caused you to move from Hims to Damascus?" Abū Sallām replied, "By Allah, you are the first Arab to ask me this question. I have heard that the blessing is doubled in it".

[*Ibn 'Asākir*]

Ibn 'Umar ﷺ reports that the Prophet ﷺ said, "A huge fire will issue from the direction of the sea of Hadramawt before the Day of Resurrection, which will cause a great movement of people". The Companions asked, "O Messenger of Allah what do you order us to do at that time?" He ﷺ replied, "You must go to al-Shām".

[*Tirmidhī*]

Mu'āwiyah ibn Haydah ﷺ reports that he asked the Prophet ﷺ, "Messenger of Allah, where do you order me to go?" "There" and he ﷺ gestured with his hand towards al-Shām.

[*Tirmidhī*]

Abū Umāmah ﷺ reports that the Prophet ﷺ said, "The Hour will not come before the best of the people of Iraq first go to al-Shām and the worst of the people of al-Shām go to Iraq". The Prophet ﷺ further said, "You (Abū Umāmah) must go to al-Shām".

[*Imām Aḥmad*]

'Abdullāh ibn 'Amr ﷺ reports that the Prophet ﷺ said, "There will be successive emigrations (towards the End of Time), at which time the best of human beings will be those who hold fast to the migration of Ibrāhīm ﷺ".

[*Sunan Abū Dāwūd*]

9 A Place of Struggle

Due to the religious significance and strategic location of the Blessed Land, it has become the focus of numerous attempts of occupation by non-Muslims. It is the obligation of all Muslims (men, women, young and old) to play a constructive role in the defence of al-Ḥaram al-Sharīf (al-Aqṣā Sanctuary). Muslims have thwarted past attempts through their unity and by showing unconditional support for the defenders of al-Aqṣā Sanctuary. Every individual from every part of the globe has a role to play and must exercise his ability for the just cause.

> The Messenger of Allah ﷺ said regarding the inhabitants of the Blessed Land, "They and their wives, children, and slaves (men and women) are in rībāṭ (guardians, literally a fort) in the cause of Allah ﷻ".
>
> [*Al-Ṭabarānī*]

> The Messenger of Allah ﷺ said, "Guarding the land of Islam for a night is better than fasting for a month and praying in its nights; and when one dies, while guarding, his deeds will keep growing till the Judgement Day and he will be protected from the turmoil of the grave".
>
> [*Ṣaḥīḥ Muslim*]

Muʿāwiyah ibn Abī Sufyān ﷺ relates that the Prophet ﷺ said, "There is a group among my followers who will continue to remain on the truth. No one who opposes them will harm them until the coming of the Hour". The Companions asked, "Where will they be?" The Messenger ﷺ replied, "They will be in and around Bayt al-Maqdis".

[*Imām Aḥmad*]

Muʿādh ibn Jabal ﷺ relates that the Prophet ﷺ said, "Allah Almighty will enable you to conquer al-Shām after my death. Their men and women will be garrisoned until the Day of Judgement. Whoever from among you chooses one of the coasts of al-Shām or al-Quds (Jerusalem) is in the sacred struggle (jihād) until the Day of Judgement".

Nahīk ibn Surīm al-Sakūnī ﷺ relates that the Prophet ﷺ said, "You will fight the pagans until the remnant of you fights on the River Jordan, you to the east of it (present-day Jordan) and they to the west of it (occupied Palestine)".

[*Ibn Ḥajar al-ʿAsqalānī*]

Abū Hurayrah ﷺ relates that the Prophet ﷺ said, "A group of my community will not cease to fight at the gates of Damascus and at the gates of al-Quds (Jerusalem) and its surroundings. The betrayal or desertion of whoever deserts them will not harm them in the least. They will remain victorious, standing for truth, until the Final Hour rises".

[*Al-Ṭabarānī*]

10 The Centre of Belief and Goodness

Abū Dardā ﷺ reports that the Prophet ﷺ said, "As I was sleeping I saw the Column of the Book being carried away from under my head. I feared lest it would be taken away, so I followed it with my eyes and saw that it was being planted in al-Shām. Verily, faith in the time of dissensions will be in al-Shām".

[*Al-Ṭabarānī*]

'Abdullāh ibn 'Amr ﷺ reports that the Prophet ﷺ repeated the above statement three times: "When the dissension takes place belief shall be in al-Shām". One version of the ḥadīth states, "Safety will be in al-Shām".

[*Al-Ṭabarānī*]

'Abdullāh ibn Hawalah ﷺ reports that the Prophet ﷺ said, "I saw on the night of al-Isrā', al-Mi'rāj (the Night Journey) a white column resembling a pearl, which the angels were carrying. I asked them, 'What are you carrying?' They replied, 'The Column of the Book, we have been ordered to place it in al-Shām'. Later in my sleep, I saw the Column of the Book was being taken away from under my headrest. I began to fear lest Allah the Almighty had abandoned the people of the earth. My eyes followed the Column of the Book. It was a brilliant light in front of me. Then I saw it was placed in al-Shām".

[Al-Ṭabarānī]

Abū Umāmah reports that the Prophet said, "Prophethood descended upon me from/in three places: Makkah, Madinah and al-Shām. Once it is brought out from any of them, it shall never return to it (Sunan Abū Dāwūd). In another version it states, "The Qur'ān was revealed in three places: Makkah, Madinah and al-Shām" (Al-Ṭabarānī). Ibn Kathīr the great scholar of Islam said, "al-Shām here means Bayt al-Maqdis".

Qurrah ibn Iyās reports that the Prophet said, "When the people of al-Shām become corrupted, no goodness will be left among you. (Yet) there will not cease to be a group in my community that will remain victorious over all people, those who betray or desert them cannot harm them in the least and so until the Final Hour comes".

[Tirmidhī]

'Abdullāh ibn Dirār reports that the Prophet said, "Goodness is in ten parts, nine in al-Shām and the one remaining for the rest. Evil is ten parts, one in al-Shām and nine for the rest. When the people in al-Shām become corrupt no goodness will be left in you".

[Al-Ṭabarānī]

11 A Place of Caliphate

Muʿādh ibn Jabal ؓ relates that the Prophet ﷺ said, "The flourishing state of al-Quds (Jerusalem) (under the non-Muslim) will be when Yathrib is in ruins, the ruined state of Yathrib will be when the *Great War* comes, the outbreak of the *Great War* will be at the conquest of Constantinople and the conquest of Constantinople will be when al-Dajjāl (Anti-Christ) comes forth. He (the Prophet ﷺ) struck his thigh or his shoulder with his hand and said: This is as true as you are here or as you are sitting (meaning Muʿādh ibn Jabal)".

[Sunan Abū Dāwūd]

ʿAbdullāh ibn Hawalah al-Azdī ؓ has reported "The Prophet ﷺ put his hand on my head and said, "Ibn Hawalah if you see that the Caliphate has taken abode in the Holy Land then the earthquakes, tribulations and great events are at hand. The Last Hour on that day will be closer to people than my hand is to your head".

[Imām Aḥmad and Sunan Abū Dāwūd]

Yūnus ibn Maysarah ؓ relates that the Prophet ﷺ said, "This matter (the Caliphate) will be after me in Madinah, then al-Shām, then al-Jazīrah, then Iraq, then in Madinah, then in al-Quds (Jerusalem). If it is in al-Quds (Jerusalem), its home country is there and if any people expel it, it will not return there forever".

[*Ibn 'Asākir*]

Al-Num'ān ibn Bashīr ﷺ relates that the Prophet ﷺ said, "Prophethood will last with you for as long as Allah ﷻ wants it. Then Allah ﷻ will end it if He wishes to end it. Then there will be the rightly guided Caliphs according to the method of Prophethood and things will be as Allah ﷻ wishes them. Then Allah ﷻ will end it if He wishes it. Then there will be a voracious kingdom and things will be as Allah ﷻ wishes them. Then Allah ﷻ will end it if He wishes. Then there will be Caliph according to the method of Prophethood". Thereafter, the Prophet ﷺ fell silent.

[*Imām Aḥmad*]

'Abd al-Raḥmān ibn abī 'Umayrah al-Muzanī ﷺ relates that the Prophet ﷺ said, "There will be an oath of allegiance according to guidance in al-Quds (Jerusalem)".

[*'Alā' al-Dīn al-Hindī*]

12 The Virtues of Praying and Charity

Ibn al-Jawzī and Abū Bakr al-Wāsiṭī stated that many scholars of Islam believe that it is not only the reward for prayers in al-Ḥaram al-Sharīf (al-Aqṣā Sanctuary) that are multiplied as compared to prayers elsewhere, but the reward for all good deeds are multiplied. Similarly, the punishments for bad deeds in this Holy area are also believed to be multiplied.

The rationale behind increasing the virtues is clearly to imbibe within the believers a sense of love, affection and a need to incline towards these Holy sites. The increased merits in praying at al-Aqṣā Sanctuary are a clear signal for the believers to frequent al-Aqṣā Sanctuary and ensure its well-being.

A. Virtues of praying

Abū Dardā' ◈ relates that the Prophet ◈ said, "A prayer in Makkah is worth 100,000 times, a prayer in my Mosque (Madinah) is worth 1,000 times, and a prayer in al-Aqṣā Sanctuary is worth 500 times, more than anywhere else".

[Al-Ṭabarānī, al-Bayhaqī and al-Suyūṭī]

'Abdullāh ibn 'Umar ؓ relates, I asked the Prophet ﷺ, "Apostle of Allah, tell us the legal injunction about (visiting) Bayt al-Maqdis (Jerusalem)." The Apostle of Allah ﷺ said, "Go and pray there. If you cannot visit it and pray there, then send some oil to be used in the lamps".

[*Ṣaḥīḥ al-Bukhārī*]

Anas ibn Mālik ؓ relates that the Prophet ﷺ said, "The prayer of a person in his house is a single prayer; his prayer in the Masjid of his tribe has the reward of twenty-five prayers; his prayer in the Masjid in which the Friday prayer is observed has the reward of five hundred; his prayer in the Masjid al-Aqṣā (i.e. al-Aqṣā Sanctuary) has a reward of five thousand prayers; his prayer in my Masjid (the Prophet's Masjid in Madinah) has a reward of fifty thousand prayers; and the prayer in the Sacred Masjid (Ka'bah) at Makkah has a reward of one hundred thousand prayers".

[*Tirmidhī and Ibn Mājah*]

Abū Dharr ؓ reported that he asked the Prophet ﷺ, "O Prophet of Allah, which Masjid was built first on earth?" The Prophet ﷺ replied, "The Sacred Masjid of Makkah". Abū Dharr again asked, "Which was next?" The Prophet ﷺ said, "The Masjid al-Aqṣā". "How long was the period between them?" Abū Dharr asked. The Prophet ﷺ said, "Forty years". Apart from these, offer your prayers anywhere when it is time to pray, although excellence is in praying in these Masajids".

[*Ṣaḥīḥ al-Bukhārī*]

B. Virtues of performing I'tikāf

If someone makes a vow to perform i'tikāf (seclusion for worship) in the Masjid al-Ḥaram (in Makkah), the Prophet's Masjid (in

Madinah), or in the Masjid al-Aqṣā (in Jerusalem), he is to fulfil his vow, as the Prophet ﷺ said: "One should not undertake journeys except to three mosques: the Masjid al-Ḥaram, the Masjid al-Aqṣā, or this Masjid (the Prophet's Masjid)".

> If someone vows to perform i'tikāf in another Masjid, it is not obligatory on him to fulfil it in that Masjid and he may perform that i'tikāf in any Masjid, for Allah ﷻ did not specify any particular place for His worship, and there is no superiority of one Masjid over another (with the exception of the three Masajids mentioned earlier). It has been confirmed that the Prophet ﷺ said: "A prayer in my Masjid is superior to one thousand prayers in any other Masjid but the Masjid al-Ḥaram (in Makkah), and a prayer in that Masjid is superior to a prayer in my Masjid by one hundred prayers".
>
> Thus, if someone makes a vow to perform i'tikāf in the Prophet's Masjid, he may fulfil it in the Masjid al-Ḥaram since that one is superior to the Prophet's Masjid.
>
> [*Fiqh al-Sunnah*]

C. Virtues of charity

This ḥadīth narrated by, Maymūnah bint Sa'd ؓ is exceptional, as it is the only ḥadīth that draws a parallel between charity and performing ṣalāh. This should encourage the believers to donate towards al-Ḥaram al-Sharīf (al-Aqṣā Sanctuary). No other similar recommendation has been made for any of the other Masajid. The Muslims are directly requested to oversee the welfare of the Masjid al-Aqṣā and make this a duty of each and everyone. The Prophet's pronouncement that assisting the Masjid al-Aqṣā coming next to performing ṣalāh there, should not be underestimated and is a clear indication for the believers to engage in the welfare of the al-Ḥaram al-Sharīf (al-Aqṣā Sanctuary).

Maymūnah bint Saʿd ؓ relates that she asked the Prophet ﷺ, "O Prophet ﷺ! Inform us about Bayt al-Maqdis (Jerusalem)". He said, "Visit it for prayer". She further asked, "If one of us cannot visit it, what should we do?" He said, "If you cannot go for prayer then send some oil to be used in its lamps; whosoever gives oil for its lamps, will be as if he has prayed in it".

[*Imām Aḥmad, Ibn Mājah, Sunan Abū Dāwūd and al-Ṭabarānī*]

(Reported also by Abū Yaʿlā; all of its narrators were classified as reliable.)

This ḥadīth is a clear indication of the high regard the Prophet Muḥammad ﷺ wished to emphasise upon the Muslims regarding Masjid al-Aqṣā.

13 Travel for Prayers

Yet again, we see the Sharī'ah teaching and encouraging us to visit al-Ḥaram al-Sharīf (al-Aqṣā Sanctuary), and thereby building in our hearts love and affection for the blessed place. The encouragement to travel towards al-Aqṣā Sanctuary is also a signal to the believer to remain informed about the Masjid al-Aqṣā, assist with its needs and increase *taqwā* by building the love for the Masjid al-Aqṣā, one of the greatest symbols of Islam.

> Abū Hurayrah ﵁ relates that the Prophet ﷺ said, "You should not undertake a special journey to visit any place other than the three Masajid with the expectations of getting greater reward: the Sacred Masjid of Makkah, this Masjid of mine, and Masjid al-Aqṣā (of Jerusalem)". In another narration the words are, "For three Masajid a special journey may be undertaken: The Sacred Masjid (Ka'bah), my Masjid, and the Masjid of al-Quds (Jerusalem)".
>
> [*Ṣaḥīḥ al-Bukhārī, Ṣaḥīḥ Muslim, and Sunan Abū Dāwūd*]

Abū Sa'īd ﵁, who participated in twelve Ghazawāt (battles) with the Prophet ﷺ, said, "I heard four things from Allah's Apostle (or I narrate them from the Prophet ﷺ) which won my admiration and appreciation". They are:

1. No lady should travel without her husband or without a Maḥram (a person you cannot marry).
2. No fasting is permissible on two days of 'Īd al-Fiṭr, and 'Īd al-Aḍḥā.
3. No prayer (may be offered) after two prayers: after the 'Aṣr prayer till sunset and after the morning prayer till sunrise.
4. Not to travel (for visiting) except for three Masajid: Masjid al-Ḥaram (in Makkah), my Masjid (in Madinah), and Masjid al-Aqṣā (in Jerusalem).

[*Ṣaḥīḥ al-Bukhārī*]

In our era of jet travel where the world has become a global village and especially for those living in the Western world, the journey to Masjid al-Aqṣā should be easy. However, it is surprising to find that despite the advice of the Prophet Muḥammad ﷺ and the ease with which one can travel most Muslims in the West have not visited Masjid al-Aqṣā. Our selective concept of dīn has subconsciously allowed us to ignore the Masjid al-Aqṣā. It is important to realize we must serve dīn as the need requires, rather than what pleases us and is simple to carry out.

14 Starting Ḥajj or ʿUmrah from Masjid al-Aqṣā

The Prophet Muḥammad ﷺ used all means possible to ensure that the Ummah does not forget al-Ḥaram al-Sharīf (al-Aqṣā Sanctuary). The most sacred journey for the Muslim is the journey of Ḥajj or ʿUmrah, and the Prophet ﷺ stated that every Muslim should consider travelling via Masjid al-Aqṣā to perform these rites. It became the norm of the pious predecessors to follow the Prophet's ﷺ advice and adorn their iḥrām in al-Ḥaram al-Sharīf (al-Aqṣā Sanctuary). The numerous references in the Sharīʿah to al-Aqṣā Sanctuary should ensure that it remains at the forefront of our concerns and also serve as a warning to the believers against neglecting it. The advice of the Prophet Muḥammad ﷺ and the tradition of the pious predecessors needs to be revived and believers need to strive and adorn the iḥrām from al-Ḥaram al-Sharīf (al-Aqṣā Sanctuary) before proceeding for Ḥajj or ʿUmrah.

> Umm Salamah ﵂, *Umm al-Muʾminīn*, relates that the Prophet ﷺ said, "If anyone puts on iḥrām for Ḥajj or ʿUmrah from the Masjid al-Aqṣā and then proceeds to the Sacred Masjid, his former and latter sins will be forgiven, or he will be guaranteed Paradise". The narrator ʿAbdullāh doubted which of these words he ﷺ said.
>
> [*Sunan Abū-Dāwūd*]

Imām Malik relates Yaḥyā ﷺ related to me from a reliable source that 'Abdullāh ibn 'Umar once entered iḥrām at Ilyā' (Jerusalem).

[*Imām Mālik*]

As stated earlier, those Companions that are known to have adorned their iḥrām from al-Aqṣā Sanctuary include: 'Umar ibn al-Khaṭṭāb ﷺ, the second righteous Caliph; Sa'd ibn Abī Waqqāṣ ﷺ; 'Abdullāh ibn 'Umar ﷺ; Tamīm al-Dārī ﷺ; 'Amr ibn al-'Āṣ ﷺ; Abū Hurayrah ﷺ; and 'Abdullāh ibn 'Abbās ﷺ.

15 Historical Significance

A. Second House of prayer on earth

The Islamic historical heritage of al-Quds (Jerusalem) dates back further than that of the Jewish or Christian. Muslims believe that Masjid al-Aqṣā was first built by Prophet Ādam عليه السلام at the beginning of human life on Earth. The ḥadīth below further shows that Masjid al-Aqṣā was built 40 years after the Ka'bah, as Prophet Ādam عليه السلام built the Ka'bah in Makkah then he moved to al-Quds (Jerusalem) and built the second house of Allah on earth, Masjid al-Aqṣā. The Ka'bah in Makkah was much later re-built by Prophet Ibrāhīm عليه السلام with his son Ismail عليه السلام, while Masjid al-Aqṣā was re-built by Prophet Ibrāhīm عليه السلام with his son Isḥāq عليه السلام. Prophet Dāwūd عليه السلام began re-construction of Masjid al-Aqṣā in his time, and this was completed by Sulaymān عليه السلام. The importance of al-Quds (Jerusalem) to Jewish and Christian people began with Prophet Ibrāhīm عليه السلام and the rebuilding of Masjid al-Aqṣā by Dāwūd عليه السلام on Mount Moriah. To Muslims, Dāwūd عليه السلام is one of the many Prophets in the chain of Prophets associated with this blessed site. Muslims believe in him and all the other Prophets mentioned in the Qur'ān.

Abū Dharr ﷺ reported that he asked the Prophet ﷺ, "O Prophet of Allah, which Masjid was built first on earth?" The Prophet ﷺ replied, "The Sacred Masjid of Makkah". Abū Dharr again asked, "Which was next?" The Prophet ﷺ said, "The Masjid al-Aqṣā". "How long was the period between them?" Abū Dharr asked. The Prophet ﷺ replied, "Forty years".

[*Ṣaḥīḥ al-Bukhārī and Ṣaḥīḥ Muslim*]

Imām Qurṭubī says "There are different opinions regarding the construction of Masjid al-Aqṣā. Some assert that Ādam عليه السلام established Masjid al-Ḥaram in Makkah and then proceeded to build Masjid al-Aqṣā 40 years later. Others assert the angels laid the foundation of Masjid al-Ḥaram and after 40 years established Masjid al-Aqṣā. There are a lot of possibilities and Allah knows best."

[*Jāmiʿ Aḥkām al-Qur'ān*]

Ibn Ḥajar ʿAsqalānī says "The first to establish the foundation of Masjid al-Aqṣā was Ādam عليه السلام, some say angels, some say Nūḥ عليه السلام and some say Dāwūd عليه السلام and I incline towards those who say Ādam عليه السلام was the first to lay the foundation of Masjid al-Aqṣā."

[*Fatḥ al-Bārī*]

B. Caliph ʿUmar

After the Muslims had defeated the Romans at the battle of Yarmūk, they converged on the blessed city of al-Quds (Jerusalem). The inhabitants of al-Quds (Jerusalem), none of whom were Jews, applied for a conditional surrender and undertook to open the gates if the Caliph ʿUmar رضي الله عنه came in person. The Muslims could have ignored the condition and taken al-Quds (Jerusalem) by force.

But, inevitably, many would have lost their lives, so to avoid unnecessary bloodshed, the Muslims complied with the conditions. Abū 'Ubaydaḥ ﷺ wrote to 'Umar ﷺ in Madinah, who duly set out for the Holy City.

'Umar ﷺ requested all the Muslim generals to meet him at al-Jābiyah (in present-day Amman). When 'Umar ﷺ entered al-Jābiyah, a Jew came up to him and said, "Peace be upon you, O Fārūq! You are the master of al-Quds (Jerusalem). By God, you will not return before God conquers al-Quds (Jerusalem)!"[9]

While the Companions were sitting at al-Jābiyah, in a spontaneous move they reached for their weapons. 'Umar ﷺ asked, "What is it?" There was a cloud of dust being raised on the horizon by a cavalry and to this the Companions directed 'Umar's attention. Cavalry brandishing swords were visible. He said, "They are seeking assurance of safety. Do not be afraid, but grant it to them". As they came closer it became apparent, they were from al-Quds (Jerusalem) requesting assurances of safety. 'Umar ﷺ wrote for them his peace condition:[10]

In the name of Allah, the Merciful, the Compassionate.

This is the assurance of safety, which the servant of Allah, 'Umar, the Commander of the Faithful, has granted to the people of Ilyā' (Jerusalem).

He has granted them an assurance of safety for their lives, properties, churches, crosses, the sick and the healthy of the city, and for all the rituals that belong to their religion. Their churches will not be inhabited by Muslims and will not be destroyed. Neither they, nor the land on which they stand, nor their crosses, nor their property will be damaged. They will not be forcibly converted. No Jew will live with them in Jerusalem.[11]

The people of al-Quds must pay *Jizyah* like the people of the other cities. As for those who will leave the city, their lives will be safe until they reach their place of safety, and as for those who remain, they will be safe. They will have to pay the *Jizyah* like the people of al-Quds. Those of the people of al-Quds who want to leave with the Byzantines, take their property, and abandon their churches and their crosses will be safe until they reach their place of safety. Those villagers who were in al-Quds before the killing of so-and-so may remain in the city if they wish, but they must pay *Jizyah* like the people of al-Quds. Those who wish may go with the Byzantines, and those who wish may return to their families. Nothing will be taken from them before their harvest is reaped. If they pay the *Jizyah* according to their obligations, then the contents of this letter are under the covenant of Allah, and are the responsibility of His Prophet, of the Caliphs, and the faithful.

The persons who attest to it are: Khālid ibn al-Walīd ﷺ, ʻAmr ibn al-ʻĀṣ ﷺ, ʻAbd al-Raḥmān ibn ʻAwf ﷺ and Muʻāwiyah ibn abī Sufyān ﷺ.

This covenant was signed in the year 15 (636-637).[12]

Al-Fārūq ﷺ, the Great Caliph, then made his epic journey but in striking contrast to King Saul, Nebuchadnezzar, Titus and Heraclius. Nebuchadnezzar and Titus desecrated and razed the whole Temple, while Saul and Heraclius brought religious fanaticism, leading to persecution and oppression.

ʻUmar ﷺ, from al-Jābiyah, in his simple patched attire mounted his horse. The Companions, on seeing the worn-out clothes and dreary tired horse, thought the Christians in al-Quds (Jerusalem) would mock him. They brought ʻUmar ﷺ a new cloak and a thoroughbred. ʻUmar ﷺ changed his clothes and mounted his ride but it soon began to sway. ʻUmar ﷺ realised that such vanity was alien to Muslims and thus dismounted and ordered them to bring him back his old horse and simple clothes. He wore these and with just one assistant, made the journey towards al-Quds (Jerusalem).

While travelling, they each took turns to ride the horse while the other walked. When the last furlong approached, it became

'Umar's turn to walk and his assistant to ride. The assistant pleaded with 'Umar ﷺ in every manner that he should continue riding as they approached al-Quds (Jerusalem), but he would not hear of it and forced his assistant to comply with the original agreement. Thus 'Umar ﷺ, on foot, with great humility and sincerity entered through the gates of the great city of al-Quds (Jerusalem) to begin the Islamic reign.

For many Jews, their prayer had been answered. Despite a condition excluding Jewish people, dictated by the Christians of al-Quds (Jerusalem) before the surrender of the city, the Muslims appear to have waived it and for the first time in over six hundred years, Jews were once again allowed to enter al-Quds (Jerusalem). seventy Jewish families found immediate accommodation within al-Quds (Jerusalem).[13]

Many Christians and pagans were also at ease as they were allowed total freedom to follow any sect they wished without fear of persecution. Thus, al-Quds (Jerusalem) was transformed into a pluralist city at a stroke.

With the modern Zionist attempts to Judaise al-Quds (Jerusalem), it is important to realise that the Muslims did not liberate al-Quds (Jerusalem) from the Jews, but rather from the Christians. But it was the Jews and other minority groups who were the major benefactors of the Muslim liberation of the city.

At the time, the Bishop, Sophronius, came to the gates to welcome 'Umar ﷺ. When he saw 'Umar ﷺ, he said, "In truth this is the abomination of the desolation established in the holy place, which Daniel ﷺ the Prophet spoke of".[14] The first request 'Umar ﷺ made was to be taken to al-Ḥaram al-Sharīf (al-Aqṣā Sanctuary). When the gates to the Holy Sanctuary were opened he turned towards the *miḥrāb* of Prophet Dāwūd ﷺ (David)[15] and prostrated the prostration of Dāwūd and thereafter performed two *rak'ah* ṣalāh[16]. In the first *rak'ah* he recited *Sūrah Ṣād,* 38 and in the next *rak'ah Sūrah Banū Isrā'īl.*

Thereafter, he called for Ka'b ﷺ and asked, "Where do you think we should establish the place of prayer (Masjid)?" Ka'b ﷺ said, "Place the Masjid behind the Rock". 'Umar ﷺ disagreed, as this would mean people having to stand behind the rock in order to face the *qiblah* and thus people might start to venerate the rock.[17] Thus 'Umar ﷺ built the Masjid with its *qiblah* in front of the rock. 'Umar ﷺ then stood up and went to the rubbish tip which the Byzantines had left in the compound of al-Aqṣā Sanctuary.

He said, "O People! Do what I am doing". He knelt down in the midst of the rubbish and gathered rubbish by the handful into the lower part of his mantle.[18] The Companions followed suit and worked throughout the day until all the rubbish accumulated by the Byzantines was cleared. 'Umar ﷺ then ordered the construction of a Masjid whereon stands today's elegant black domed Masjid al-Aqṣā.

It appears that Sophronius and 'Umar ﷺ built a cordial relationship. Sophronius offered 'Umar ﷺ a robe and a loincloth as a gift. However, 'Umar ﷺ refused. On the persistence of the Bishop, 'Umar ﷺ compromised and said, "I shall wear your clothes while mine are sent for washing". When 'Umar ﷺ received his clothes back, he returned the robe to the Bishop. On one occasion when the Bishop was giving 'Umar ﷺ a tour of al-Quds (Jerusalem), the time for prayer – ṣalāh – approached when they were in the Church of the Holy Sepulchre. The Bishop offered 'Umar ﷺ the opportunity to perform his ṣalāh in the church but 'Umar ﷺ, with foresight and humility, declined. He feared that if he performed his ṣalāh in the church it might be that future generations of Muslims, on the pretext of following in his footsteps, would also enter the church to perform ṣalāh and that this could lead to inconvenience, harassment and possible confiscation of the Church.

'Umar ﷺ spent a few weeks[19] in al-Quds (Jerusalem), attending to state, civil and personal matters before returning with the utmost simplicity to Madinah.

C. Tamīm al-Dārī

Tamīm al-Dārī was a knowledgeable Christian from Palestine who travelled to Madinah in 9 AH (631) in order to meet the Prophet Muḥammad ﷺ after having heard about his mission. After meeting the Prophet ﷺ, Tamīm al-Dārī accepted Islam and some time later he asked the Prophet ﷺ to grant him an area around al-Khalīl (Hebron) once the Muslims liberated Palestine. The Prophet ﷺ signed a document granting Tamīm al-Dārī an area around al-Khalīl as *waqf* (religious endowment), with the condition that this land could not be sold to anyone. Tamīm al-Dārī presented the Prophet's document to 'Umar when the Muslims liberated al-Quds (Jerusalem). 'Umar granted Tamīm the promised area around Hebron but after dividing it into three parts: one-third for Tamīm and his family; a second third for the poor, wayfarers and travellers; and the last third to be built on by the people.[20] Maḥmūd Ibrāhīm in *Faḍā'il al-Quds* (Virtues of Jerusalem), states that Tamīm became the governor of al-Quds (Jerusalem) after the reign of Caliph 'Uthmān.

The Prophet's practice of assigning land as *waqf* was followed by many other Caliphs, which led to great areas of the Holy Land and in particular al-Quds (Jerusalem), being bequeathed as *waqf*. The *waqf*, or religious endowment land, cannot be sold nor can its ownership be transferred.

Imām al-Ghazālī gave a fatwā that indicated that: "Anyone who questions the correctness of this bequest and opposes it is an unbeliever".

It is extremely important to note the conviction and total belief of the Ṣaḥābah in the Prophet Muḥammad's ﷺ promise that al-Quds would be liberated, even though at the time even Makkah was under the control of non-believers. It was this faith which ensured the liberation of not only al-Quds but the entire al-Shām.

D. Bilāl ibn Rabāḥ ؓ

As mentioned above, during 'Umar's ؓ stay in al-Quds (Jerusalem), the *adhān* is said to have been called by Bilāl ibn Rabāḥ ؓ, the first *muezzin* in Islam (also called the Prophet's ﷺ *muezzin*). 'Umar ؓ requested Bilāl ؓ to give the *adhān*, and he complied even though he had vowed never to call the *adhān* after the Holy Prophet's ﷺ demise. When the Companions heard his inspiring voice, vivid memories of the Golden Era in Madinah with the beloved Prophet ﷺ came flooding back and many burst into tears.

E. Building of Masjid al-Aqṣā

As stated above, the first request Caliph 'Umar ؓ made upon entering al-Quds (Jerusalem) was to be taken to al-Ḥaram al-Sharīf (al-Aqṣā Sanctuary). When he arrived there, he was laden with sorrow to see that the Romans had been using the Holy Sanctuary as a rubbish tip. After himself initiating the clearance of the site, he ordered the construction of a Masjid at the southern end of the sanctuary. This was originally a wooden structure and was later rebuilt as a solid structure by 'Abd al-Malik's son al-Walīd (Caliph 705-715). Today, the black dome of Masjid al-Aqṣā stands there.

It is important to note that to Muslims, it is the area of land that comprises al-Ḥaram al-Sharīf (al-Aqṣā Sanctuary) which is more important than any of the structures on it, as Allah ؑ has "blessed the land". The buildings are also important by virtue of being on blessed land and for their respective historical links but it is the land that is of paramount importance.

F. Qubbat al-Ṣakhrah (Dome of the Rock)

The Umayyad Caliph, 'Abd al-Malik ibn Marwān commissioned the building of the Qubbat al-Ṣakhrah (Dome of the Rock) in

72-73 AH (691-692). The reason for building this architectural wonder of the world has drawn many hypotheses. However, to most Muslims it is logical for such an endeavour of magnificence to have taken place in al-Quds (Jerusalem). As it is the site of the most miraculous event in the life of the Prophet Muḥammad ﷺ – al-Isrā' and al-Mi'rāj – coupled with the many aḥādīth exalting the virtues of al-Aqṣā Sanctuary and the fact that it is mentioned in the Holy Qur'ān. Renowned jurist 'Abd al-Malik, must have been aware of all these and to commemorate the Islamic heritage of the area, undertook the grand project of building the magnificent dome over the rock.

It may also be conceivable that when 'Abd al-Malik entered al-Quds (Jerusalem), the prominent buildings of Christians, in particular the Church of the Holy Sepulchre built by Emperor Constantine, initiated a desire to construct an Islamic building to surpass those of the conquered people. Historians like al-Maqdisī have supported this theory.

There is a bankrupt academic theory proposed by al-Ya'qūbi, who was against the Umayyad's, which has gained currency amongst contemporary Orientalist scholars. This was the view that 'Abd al-Malik sought to divert the Ḥajj from Makkah to al-Quds (Jerusalem) and thus built the Qubbat al-Ṣakhrah. They base their argument on the fact that at the time 'Abdullāh ibn Zubayr had gained control of Makkah and become a counter Caliph, he denied access to the Umayyads. It suffices to state, that such an incredible claim emanates from only those with absolutely no knowledge of Islam or those clutching at straws in order to plant controversy within Muslim minds and attempt to undermine Islamic heritage. It is obvious that any individual, even if he happens to be a Caliph, who directs Muslims to perform Ḥajj, which is *farḍ* (compulsory duty) and the fifth pillar of Islam, away from its rightful place would immediately become a *kāfir* against whom the entire Ummah would wage jihād. Hence this theory can be discarded without giving it a second thought.

G. The Crusaders

The Crusades were a series of campaigns against the Muslim world, which started in 1095 and lasted until the fall of Acre in 1291.

The bloodthirsty Pope Urban II, called his Christian brethren to arm themselves in order to march upon the "Saracens" (a derogatory term for Arabs and Muslims) and liberate al-Quds (Jerusalem) from the "infidels". With the promise of heaven and, more importantly, great booty from the Muslim world, Europeans rallied to Urban's cry in their thousands.

The Crusaders, as they were known, converged on Constantinople (Istanbul) *en route* to the Holy Land and they killed all who disagreed with their mission.

The European force joined with the Byzantine army and sallied forth towards their objective, capturing major cities on the way.

It was on Friday 15 July 1099, that the Crusading Europeans arrived at the gates of al-Quds (Jerusalem). They began a siege, which lasted 6 weeks, and the city eventually fell. Led by Tancred, the Crusaders smashed their way into the Qubbat al-Ṣakhrah (Dome of the Rock) and stripped it of all the gold and silver within. The Muslims fled into the other great Masjid – the black domed Masjid al-Aqṣā – before surrendering and agreeing to pay a ransom to Tancred, whose word turned out to be worthless. The very next morning the Crusaders re-entered Masjid al-Aqṣā and slaughtered each and every person there. No one really knows how many were butchered but historians estimate that over 70,000 people died. One of the Crusaders spoke of struggling to walk through a mass of blood and bodies more than knee-high.

The Crusaders then turned their attention to the Jews and locked them in their synagogues before burning them, and all the occupants, to the ground.

Under Crusader rule no Muslim or Jew was permitted to reside in al-Quds (Jerusalem). The Qubbat al-Ṣakhrah (Dome of the Rock) was re-named *Templum Domini* and had a cross placed on top of the golden dome. Al-Aqṣā Masjid was re-named *Templum Solomonis*.

The Crusaders didn't stop at robbing every living Muslim in al-Quds (Jerusalem); after accumulating all that was visible they turned their greedy attention to the dead. Fulcher of Chartres wrote, "Our squires and footmen split open the bellies of those they had slain in order to extract from the intestine the gold coins which the Saracens had gulped down their loathsome throats while alive…With drawn sword our men ran through the city not sparing anyone, even those begging for mercy…They entered the houses of the citizens, seizing whatever they found…Whoever first entered a house, was to occupy and own the house or palace and whatever found in it was as if it were entirely his own…In this way many poor crusaders became wealthy".

H. Ṣalāḥ al-Dīn al-Ayyūbī

One of the greatest generals the world has ever seen was born in Iraq in 1138, and brought up and educated in Damascus. In 1164 the Sulṭān Nūr al-Dīn sent Shirkūḥ to subdue Egypt, accompanied by Shirkūḥ's nephew, Ṣalāḥ al-Dīn. Their expedition was successful, although, thereafter, Shirkūḥ died and Ṣalāḥ al-Dīn was made the *Wazīr* (governor). When Nūr al-Dīn died in 1174, he left behind his 11-year-old son as his heir. The young man was manipulated by his none-too-faithful courtiers so Ṣalāḥ al-Dīn returned to Damascus and took over the reigns of power.

In 1187, Ṣalāḥ al-Dīn confronted the Crusaders led by Reginald at Ḥiṭṭīn, near Lake Tiberius in northern Palestine. The Crusaders suffered a crushing defeat and the road to al-Quds (Jerusalem) lay open before the victorious Ṣalāḥ al-Dīn, who entered the Holy

City peacefully on 2 October 1187. His generosity knew no bounds, for he not only let all the surviving Crusaders go free, but also gave many of them provisions for their journey home.

With al-Quds (Jerusalem) under Muslim rule once more, the Christians from Europe were free and safe to visit holy places throughout the Middle East. As the European pilgrims returned to their homes, they brought with them tales of an advanced Islamic culture with a sophisticated lifestyle and great wealth.

Ṣalāḥ al-Dīn brought with him a *mimbar*, which was commissioned by Nūr al-Dīn and placed in the Masjid al-Aqṣā. It remained there for centuries until a Zionist arson attack destroyed this beautiful masterpiece of Islamic heritage in 1969.

I. Ottoman rule (1516-1917 AD)

Palestine, like other Arab countries, was under the rule of the Ottoman Caliphate after they defeated the Mamluks. Ottoman rule lasted around four hundred years. In the beginning of the Ottoman rule, al-Quds (Jerusalem) prospered. Ottoman Sulṭāns renovated many buildings within al-Ḥaram al-Sharīf (al-Aqṣā Sanctuary). They annexed to it many prayer halls, domes, buildings, gates and fountains. However, Palestine later suffered as a result of the general decline of the empire. Nevertheless, al-Aqṣā Sanctuary is indeed a museum of Islamic architecture from the Umayyad to the Ottoman times.

J. British rule

From 1917 to 1947, the British took over the control of Palestine under a mandate from the League of Nations and no restoration or extension took place to any of the buildings within al-Ḥaram al-Sharīf (al-Aqṣā Sanctuary) during this period.

K. Jordanian rule

From 1948 to 1967, the British - created state of Jordan took control of al-Ḥaram al-Sharīf (al-Aqṣā Sanctuary). Internal politics were at play, as King 'Abdullāh wanted to represent himself to the Muslim world as the custodian of Islamic heritage. Not much religious activity or progress took place during this phase.

L. Israeli Occupation

In 1967, the Israelis occupied al-Ḥaram al-Sharīf (al-Aqṣā Sanctuary) and, unfortunately, since then the dangers to al-Ḥaram al-Sharīf (al-Aqṣā Sanctuary) have escalated. To blow up Masjid al-Aqṣā and replace it with a Jewish Temple had been the ideology of a few radicals and extreme fundamentalist Jewish groups but since the occupation of East Jerusalem in 1967, this idea has been supported by significant members of the Israeli community and Christian Zionists. A survey published after Israeli Premier Rabin's assassination in 1997 reports that 93 per cent from a sample of 1,500 Jews questioned consider al-Ḥaram al-Sharīf (al-Aqṣā Sanctuary – Temple Mount) a very important part of al-Quds (Jerusalem). Eighty-four per cent said it was important to them to be able to pray at al-Ḥaram al-Sharīf (al-Aqṣā Sanctuary) and 70 per cent were not prepared to give control of al-Aqṣā Sanctuary to the Muslims.

The report warns Muslims, "The results indicate how important the Temple Mount is to Israeli Jews. The Palestinians should be aware of these results so that they can appreciate just how great a sacrifice an Israeli compromise on the position of the Temple Mount would be for the Israeli public [sic]".

There are numerous organisations whose sole aim and purpose is to mobilise a national will and international political acceptance to blow up the buildings within al-Ḥaram al-Sharīf (al-Aqṣā Sanctuary). In 2000, seven of these fundamentalist groups joined together to form an umbrella organisation called The United Association of Movements for the Holy Temple [UAMHT], headed by Hillel Weiss, an extremist professor at Bar-llan University in Occupied Palestine. The only other fundamentalist group not to join the UAMHT was Gershom Salomon's, "The Temple Mount Faithful".

These groups are gripped in a frenzy of hate and ardent desire to blow up the buildings within al-Ḥaram al-Sharīf (al-Aqṣā Sanctuary) and every afternoon they hold a demonstration outside the Old City's Lion's Gate. Moshe Feiglin, the organiser of these daily demonstrations, is reported as saying, "Everything will stand or fall on this issue. If you give up the Temple Mount of your free will, you give up your identity – you commit spiritual suicide. There's a large majority behind us on this issue that doesn't want to disconnect from the dream of generations. Unfortunately, the majority is being overcome by a small minority that don't want to be Jews".

Salomon's group, which was formed in 1967 after the occupation of al-Ḥaram al-Sharīf (al-Aqṣā Sanctuary) by Israel, is in the forefront of many activities. On 22 July 1999 a large demonstration was organised with the purpose of entering al-Ḥaram al-Sharīf (al-Aqṣā Sanctuary) and in their words, "to remove the abomination from the Temple Mount".

On 27 September 1999, with the aid of thousands of people and the support of the Israeli establishment, they approached the Western gate of al-Ḥaram al-Sharīf (al-Aqṣā Sanctuary) in order to once again enter the al-Ḥaram al-Sharīf and lay a cornerstone foundation, weighing 4.5 tons. Only with great difficulty did the Palestinians manage to repel them. However, Salomon delivered a sermon in which he warned the Muslims that the foundation stone was ready for their Temple and it is only a matter of time before they demolish the buildings within al-Ḥaram al-Sharīf (al-Aqṣā Sanctuary) and replace it with their Temple.

On his website Salomon states, "The rebuilding of the Temple is a key event in the life of Israel which will complete the Zionist revolution on the Temple Mount. We want to bring the God of Israel into the midst of the life of the people of Israel and the world. God is ready for this and He has shown it again and again over the last 57 years. Now we must be ready to fulfil our part with great dedication to the God of Israel, to the holy land and to the Temple Mount. We must remove the foreigners [Muslims] and their terrible abomination [buildings in al-Aqṣā Sanctuary] from the hill of God to purify the place".

These groups have been openly raising funds in Israel, the USA and Europe. *Israel Wire* reported that the fundraising activities of these groups are being stepped up in order to reconstruct the Temple. The fundamentalist groups proudly proclaim the accumulation of their funds for purchasing and making Temple utensils as specified according to their understanding. For the indoctrination of the worldview in accordance to their desires they call international education campaigns. They have architectural plans and a collection of gold for their altar, "We are saving the donation of gold, silver and other jewellery for the Temple. This will be used when the construction of the Temple begins. Much gold and silver will be required for all the parts of the Temple". One of their main aims for collecting funds is claimed to be the removal of the Muslims and the buildings within the al-Ḥaram al-Sharīf (al-Aqṣā Sanctuary) from what they call the Temple Mount.

Ha'aretz, one of the leading newspapers in Occupied Palestine, in its edition of 1 March 1998 reported that an ultra-orthodox sect is searching for parents willing to hand over newborn sons, to be raised in isolation in preparation for the rebuilding of the Temple. "The idea is to raise a child, who, from the moment of birth, will not touch the dead, not be under the same roof with the dead and will not even be in hospital where the dead are also found". Once the boys turn 13 they will be able to slaughter and burn a sacred red heifer, literally a holy cow and sprinkle its ashes on people in purification ritual.

The red heifers have been genetically engineered and American Christian Zionists are leading the way. Clyde Lott of Canaan Land Restoration claims to have shipped planeloads of red cattle since 1998 to Israel, 140 heifers per load. They request a donation of US$1,000 as a gift to the non-profit corporation for their project from their sympathisers.

The Christian Zionists raise millions of dollars yearly for Israel and people like Salomon are welcomed in hundreds of churches throughout America to raise funds. Many Christian Zionists appreciate that the destruction of the buildings within al-Ḥaram al-Sharīf (al-Aqṣā Sanctuary) may trigger wars but they seem to welcome this, saying, "Christians will be spared any sufferings because they will be *raptured* and wafted up into heaven to view the slaughter below".

The view of possible wars is also welcomed by fundamentalist Jews believing that from this Israel will emerge the victor with a leadership that will realise the dream of Eretza Israel (Greater Israel).

Amongst "Torah" Jews, whose ideas the fundamentalists now drown, the belief is that the Temple can only be built after the Messiah arrives. However, the zealots who claim that the presence of the Messiah is not necessary and blowing up the buildings within al-Ḥaram al-Sharīf (al-Aqṣā Sanctuary) will hasten the coming of the Messiah, have the upper hand. The Jewish fundamentalists point to the silence of many in the political and religious leadership as an indication of their tacit approval for the project. They quote many Rabbis, including the former chief Rabbis of Israel, Mordechai Eliyahu and Shlomo Green who is quoted as saying, "I hereby notify that because of the danger of a takeover of the Temple Mount by Muslims and despite Halachic rules, it is not only permitted but it is a holy commandment to go up to the Temple

Mount. In order to protect the Temple it is permitted to enter even the Holy of Holies. So much so to enter the Temple Mount in order to stop an Arab takeover and protect our sovereignty, it is permitted and a commandment".

Rabbi Levi is quoted as saying that in order to conquer the Temple Mount from the hands of the enemy, the impurity is nullified and one can enter. The few Rabbis who still oppose the fundamentalist ideologies are under pressure and are being silenced by people like Professor Weiss of UAMHT who is collecting signatures of prominent Rabbis who say that Jewish prayer is allowed, and should be encouraged, on al-Ḥaram al-Sharīf (al-Aqṣā Sanctuary). To sneer and belittle other Jews, the fundamentalists state, "It is much easier to wait for the messiah, and thus put the blame on him, than to take the responsibility for ourselves, for our lives, for our actions. But a careful Biblical analysis and study will reveal that waiting for the messiah's arrival to begin rebuilding the Temple is just a convenient excuse".

The Israeli government has placed no restrictions upon these groups which are now gaining widespread support within Israel for their sinister ambitions and plots. Since the Israeli occupation of al-Ḥaram al-Sharīf (al-Aqṣā Sanctuary) in 1967, no Israeli has served in prison for any considerable length of time for the hundreds of violations, desecrations, plots and plans to blow up the Masjid al-Aqṣā. These are clear indications that the government, if not in direct support of these groups, at least sympathise with them and would also like to see the buildings within al-Aqṣā Sanctuary destroyed. On 24 July 1997, the Israeli courts – for the first time – allowed the fundamentalists to pray on al-Ḥaram al-Sharīf (al-Aqṣā Sanctuary).

Internationally, it is rumoured that Israel is being pushed to hand over the sovereignty of al-Ḥaram al-Sharīf (al-Aqṣā Sanctuary) to the UN Security Council. *Ha'aretz* newspaper reported that among those involved are the governments of the US, Egypt, France and UN Secretary General Kofi Annan.

However, the extremist Salomon of the Temple Mount Faithful warns, "I don't believe that Jewish life can continue to exist without the Temple Mount. The moment such an agreement is signed, I am sure that tens of thousands or even hundreds of thousands of Israelis and Jews from around the world will go up to the Temple Mount. We will force our way in to pray and we will refuse to move, we will stop the agreement with our bodies. If necessary, we will give our lives".

To many observers the storming of al-Ḥaram al-Sharīf (al-Aqṣā Sanctuary) by Ariel Sharon on the 28 September 2000 which, by January 2006 led to the martyrdom of over 4,500 Palestinians and 60,000 with injuries, was a clear signal of Sharon's support of solidarity with those planning the destruction of al-Ḥaram al-Sharīf (al-Aqṣā Sanctuary). It is also a further challenge to the Muslim Ummah's resolve and their claim to love al-Ḥaram al-Sharīf (al-Aqṣā Sanctuary).

Some of the attacks on al-Ḥaram al-Sharīf since the Israeli occupation

1967 Jewish zealots begin prayers within al-Ḥaram al-Sharīf (al-Aqṣā Sanctuary), despite the prohibition by the Chief Rabbanate of Jews of even setting a foot in it (for fear of violating its sanctity according to Judaic law).

1969 The Masjid al-Aqṣā set on fire. Entire south wing burnt down including the precious *Mimbar* (pulpit) of Nūr al-Dīn, commissioned 700 years ago and installed by the great Muslim hero Ṣalāḥ al-Dīn al-Ayyūbī. The man found guilty had sought refuge in a kibbutz and was set free after receiving psychiatric counselling.

1970	Members of the "Temple Mount Faithful" group, dedicated to demolishing buildings within al-Ḥaram al-Sharīf (al-Aqṣā Sanctuary), forcibly entered al-Aqṣā Sanctuary. They were repulsed by the Muslims who suffered casualties from Israeli troops' gunfire.
1976	Israeli Courts passed a law permitting Jews to pray in al-Ḥaram al-Sharīf (al-Aqṣā Sanctuary). After much rioting, this was revoked.
September 1979	Jewish extremists blocked one of the entrances to al-Ḥaram al-Sharīf (al-Aqṣā Sanctuary) on Friday, pointing guns at worshippers.
From 1980s	Harassment and acts of sabotage escalated. In August 1981 an Israeli helicopter hovered at low altitude over al-Ḥaram al-Sharīf (al-Aqṣā Sanctuary) preventing worshippers inside from hearing the Khuṭbah (sermon). This form of harassment is now routinely employed.
1981	Tunnels discovered under al-Ḥaram al-Sharīf (al-Aqṣā Sanctuary). World condemnation followed. These tunnels weaken the foundation of the buildings within the al-Ḥaram al-Sharīf (al-Aqṣā Sanctuary) and there is a real fear that the Masjid al-Aqṣā may soon collapse.
May 1981	The *adhān* (call to Muslim prayer) was prohibited from the minăret overlooking the Western Wall because of Jewish celebrations.
April 1982	A parcel with a fake bomb and a threat signed by Jewish extremists was discovered at one of the gates to the Sanctuary.
April 1982	An ex-Israeli army officer opened fire, killing two Muslims and filling the interior and exterior of the Qubbat al-Ṣakhrah (Dome of the Rock) with bullet marks.

June 1982	An Israeli was arrested and then released for trying to blow up buildings within al-Ḥaram al-Sharīf (al-Aqṣā Sanctuary).
1982	Jewish fundamentalists attempted to enter al-Aqṣā Sanctuary with leaflets inciting Jews to take over al-Ḥaram al-Sharīf.
January 1983	The Temple Mount Fund was established in Israel, Europe and America to raise funds for rebuilding the Jewish Temple on the site of Masjid al-Aqṣā.
March 1983	Explosives discovered at an entrance gate and four armed Israelis were discovered attempting to enter al-Aqṣā Sanctuary. Six months later they were acquitted in Israeli courts.
January 1984	Armed Jews attempted to climb the walls of al-Aqṣā Sanctuary with ladders in the middle of the night, armed with ammunitions.
1984	Armed Israeli guards start patrolling within al-Ḥaram al-Sharīf (al-Aqṣā Sanctuary). Their behaviour and presence is inimical to the sanctity of the Muslim holy site.
June 1988	Israeli troops stormed al-Ḥaram al-Sharīf (al-Aqṣā Sanctuary), firing tear gas at groups of worshippers.
July 1988	Further tunnels discovered which sparked further unrest.
October 1990	Israeli troops opened fire on worshippers in al-Ḥaram al-Sharīf (al-Aqṣā Sanctuary), killing 22 Palestinians and wounding hundreds.
March 1996	Israelis re-opened a tunnel under al-Ḥaram al-Sharīf (al-Aqṣā Sanctuary), resulting in confrontations, which resulted in the death of more than 70 Palestinians.

The excavations under al-Aqṣā Sanctuary are causing dangerous cracks in buildings adjoining the

	Western Wall. Archaeologists believe that the tunnels have weakened the building structures within the Noble Sanctuary. It is believed that a slight earth tremor, which this area is prone to, will cause al-Aqṣā Sanctuary to collapse. Many are of the opinion that this is one of the main reasons of the Zionists for digging tunnels under al-Aqṣā Sanctuary.
March 1997	Birth of a red heifer celebrated by Israelis as a sign from God to destroy buildings within al-Ḥaram al-Sharīf (al-Aqṣā Sanctuary). This is to be accomplished when the heifer is 3 years old, coinciding with March 2000. However it was claimed an impurity in the form of a white spot was later discovered on the heifer. Hence they still wait for the birth of a pure red heifer, even if it is with the assistance of genetic engineering.
October 1997	Zionist attempt to lay a 4.5 ton rock as a cornerstone for the foundation of their Temple was repulsed.
May 1999	A book is published claiming that the Ark of the Covenant (a box containing the scrolls of Jewish Law from the time of Prophet Mūsā ﷺ) is buried under al-Aqṣā Sanctuary and should be retrieved. This theory is contrary to all modern scholarly research.
September 2000	Sharon storms into al-Aqṣā Sanctuary provoking Muslims to react which has already led to the martyrdom of over 3,300 and 50,000 injured Palestinian Muslims.
2000–2006	The harassment of worshippers continues unabated. There are now restrictions on who is allowed to enter al-Ḥaram al-Sharīf; those between the age of 20 to 50 are normally denied entry and the others are let in at the discretion – entirely arbitrary – of Israeli Police who control the entrances to al-Ḥaram al-Sharīf.

16 Prophesied and Land of Promise

It is an amazing reality that the Prophet Muḥammad ﷺ was giving the glad tidings of the liberation of al-Quds (Jerusalem) to his Companions at a time when it appeared their very own survival was in doubt. At the Battle of the Trench, when the Companions were weak, hungry and facing a mighty Arab force, the Prophet ﷺ informed his Companions that al-Quds (Jerusalem) would be liberated. Similarly, at the battle of Tabūk, when the Muslims were out to check the Romans, the Prophet ﷺ talked about the liberation of al-Shām. The Prophet's ﷺ prophecies left a lasting mark on the Companions and a duty to fulfil.

'Awf ibn Mālik ؓ relates: 'I went to the Prophet ﷺ during the Battle of Tabūk while he was sitting in a leather tent. He said, "Count six signs 'Awf, between now and the approach of the Hour (Qiyāmah/Doomsday): my death; the conquest of al-Quds (Jerusalem); a plague that will afflict you (and kill you in great numbers) as the plague that afflicts sheep; the increase of wealth to such an extent that even if one is given one hundred Dīnārs he will not be satisfied; then an affliction which no Arab house will escape; and then a truce between you and Banū al-Aṣfar (i.e. the Byzantines) who will betray you and attack you under eighty flags. Under each flag will be twelve thousand soldiers".

[*Ṣaḥīḥ al-Bukhārī*]

Shaddād ibn Aws ﷺ reports that the Prophet ﷺ said, "Al-Shām will be conquered and al-Quds (Jerusalem) will be conquered and you or your sons will be Imāms there, if Allah ﷻ wills".

[*Al-Ṭabarānī*]

True to the prophecy, Shaddād ibn Aws' children did become the Imāms of Masjid al-Aqṣā.

Abū Zuhayr ﷺ reports that he heard Allah's Apostle saying, "Yemen will be conquered and some people will migrate (from Madinah) and will urge their families and those who will obey them to migrate (to Yemen) although Madinah will be better for them; if they but knew. Al-Shām will also be conquered and some people will migrate (from Madinah) and will urge their families and those who will obey them, to migrate (to Shām) although Madinah will be better for them; if they but knew. Iraq will be conquered and some people will migrate (from Madinah) and will urge their families and those who will obey them to migrate (to Iraq) although Madinah will be better for them; if they but knew".

[*Ṣaḥīḥ al-Bukhārī*]

Mu'ādh ibn Jabal ﷺ relates that the Prophet ﷺ said, "Allah Almighty will enable you to conquer al-Shām after my death. Their men and women will be garrisoned until the Day of Judgement. Whoever from among you chooses one of the coast of al-Shām or al-Quds (Jerusalem) is in the sacred struggle (jihād) until the Day of Judgement".

In 5 AH (627 CE), a pagan Arab force, 10,000 strong, and their allies gathered to attack the Muslims in Madinah. The Muslims, in order to protect themselves, decided to dig a trench around Madinah to stop the advancing force.

Salmān al-Fārisī ﵁, a Companion of the Prophet ﷺ reports, "I was working with a pick-axe in the trench where a rock gave me much trouble. The Apostle who was near saw me hacking and saw how difficult the place was. He dropped down into the trench and took the pick-axe from my hand and gave such a blow that lightning showed on impact. This happened on three consecutive occasions". I said, "O Prophet of Allah, what is the meaning of these sparks?" He said, "Did you really see that, Salmān? The first means that Allah has opened Yemen; the second al-Shām; and the third, the east".

As stated earlier, even when the Muslims were facing difficulties the Prophet ﷺ was giving the glad tidings to the Companions of the liberation of al-Shām.

It is of equal significance to note that when the first verse of *Sūrah* 17 was revealed in Makkah, the Ka'bah was littered with around 360 idols and was a place of congregation for the pagans. At the same time al-Ḥaram al-Sharīf (al-Aqṣā Sanctuary) was used as a rubbish dump by the Romans. Despite one being a place of spiritual impurity and the other physical impurity, Allah the Almighty, the All Knowing, the Creator, refers in verse 17: 1 to the Ka'bah as the Masjid Ḥaram and to al-Aqṣā as a Masjid.

This is a clear indication that despite the sorry state of these blessed and holy sites caused by human beings, to Allah the Almighty they have always been, and will always be, His Masājid.

17 Guide and Plan of al-Ḥaram al-Sharīf

The city of al-Quds now extends over an area of 45 square km. Within al-Quds is the 'old city' where major historical events took place and within the old city on the southeast corner, is the area referred to as al-Ḥaram al-Sharīf (al-Aqṣā Sanctuary). The whole area of al-Ḥaram al-Sharīf (al-Aqṣā Sanctuary) is approximately 35 acres and within this area, at the southern end, is the black domed Masjid called Masjid al-Aqṣā. In the centre lies the golden domed Masjid, Qubbat al-Ṣakhrah (Dome of the Rock) and there are within al-Ḥaram al-Sharīf, 42 other monuments and buildings, 25 water wells for drinking water and several water fountains. The wall surrounding al-Ḥaram al-Sharīf (al-Aqṣā Sanctuary) has 14 gates. Ten of these gates are open while the other 4 are closed. Al-Ḥaram al-Sharīf (al-Aqṣā Sanctuary) has 4 minarets. There are paved floors which were, and some still are, used by Sufis for dhikr and teaching.

It is extremely important to appreciate that it is the land of al-Ḥaram al-Sharīf (al-Aqṣā Sanctuary) that is most precious and blessed. Although the buildings within the noble sanctuary like the black domed Masjid al-Aqṣā and gold domed Qubbat al-Ṣakhrah (Dome of the Rock) are of great historical significance one must not lose sight of the fact that it is the land that is holy and blessed.

From the time that the great Caliph ʿUmar ﷺ arrived at the site of al-Ḥaram al-Sharīf (al-Aqṣā Sanctuary) and laid the foundation of today's black domed Masjid al-Aqṣā, to the present day, many Muslim scholars, leaders and ordinary pious individuals have continued to construct different structures within this great blessed area. Needless to say, many more pious men and women have dedicated themselves to the renovation and security of this blessed place.

The various domes, wells and colleges commemorate various Prophets, scholars and leaders associated with al-Aqṣā Sanctuary. However, these structures do not imply that a Prophet or an individual specifically identifies with the spot corresponding to the dome or well. For instance, the Dome of Mūsā recalls Prophet Mūsā's عليه السلام association with al-Aqṣā Sanctuary as does the Dome of Sulaymān and hence, the Dome of Miʿrāj (Ascension) is again to remind us of this miraculous journey rather than indicate the exact spot from where the Miʿrāj took place.

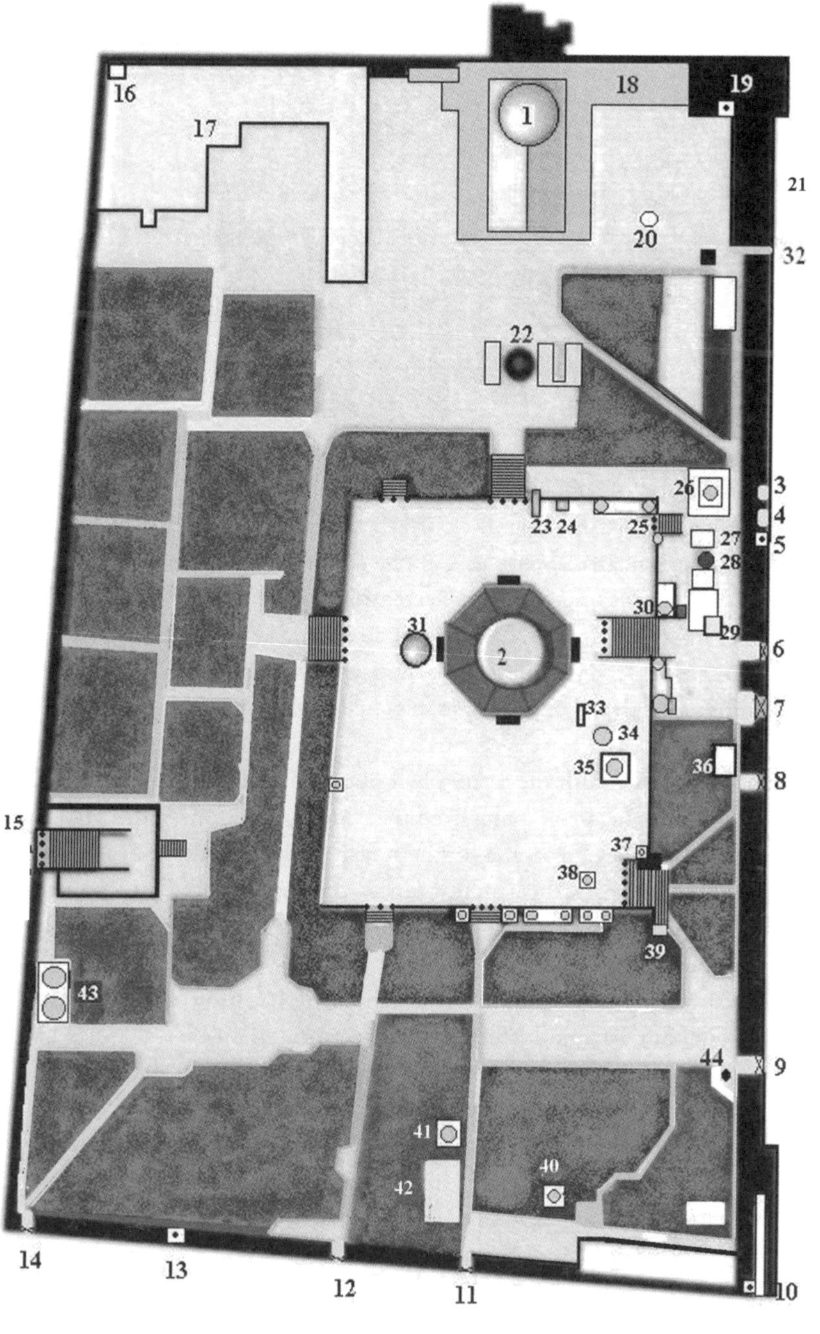
1
2
3
4
5
6
7
8
9
10
11
12
13
14
15
16
17
18
19
20
21
22
23
24
25
26
27
28
29
30
31
32
33
34
35
36
37
38
39
40
41
42
43
44

1. Masjid al-Aqṣā

A Masjid of timber was originally built here by the Great Caliph of Islam, 'Umar ﵁, in 638 (17 AH). In 691 (72 AH) 'Abd al-Malik ibn Marwān, the Umayyad Caliph, commissioned the building of the Dome over the Rock, an extension to the Masjid al-Aqṣā was undertaken by his son al-Walīd. The Masjid at the time was large enough to accommodate five thousand worshippers. It must be emphasised that the whole area is sacred to the Muslims, not just the buildings.

Directly beneath the eastern half of the Masjid al-Aqṣā building is a subterranean area, leading from the courtyard in front of the Masjid to the Double Gate in the southern wall of the Sanctuary. Sealed for hundreds of years, this gate led to the Umayyad Palaces, which once lay to the south. This area has also been opened as a place of worship by Palestinians against the wishes of Israelis.

Al-Aqṣā Masjid has been a centre of learning and worship throughout Islamic history. It has been modified several times to protect it from earthquakes which sometimes occur in the area and to adapt to the changing needs of the local population.

The form of the present structure has remained essentially the same since it was reconstructed by the Caliph al-Ẓāhir in 1033. It is said that he did not alter it from the previous architecture except to narrow it on each side.

2. Qubbat al-Ṣakhrah (Dome of the Rock)

Jerusalem became known as al-Quds (The purest place). Many of the Prophet's Companions travelled to worship at the blessed precincts from which area the Prophet Muḥammad ﷺ was brought by night and from where he ascended through the seven heavens.

In the 690s (72 AH) the Umayyad Caliph, ʻAbd al-Malik ibn Marwān, commissioned work to build a dome over the rock. Essentially unchanged for more than fourteen centuries, the Qubbat al-Ṣakhrah (Dome of the Rock) remains one of the world's most beautiful and enduring architectural treasures.

The gold Dome stretches 20m across the rock, rising to an apex of more than 35m above it. The *Sūrah Yā Sīn* is inscribed across the top in the dazzling tile work commissioned in the 16th century by Sulaymān the Magnificent. The interior is exquisitely decorated; the two most important decorative elements are the glass mosaics and the carved marble.

Under the rock is a miḥrāb (niche/cave), which visitors can view via a few steps. No one is really certain which Prophet, if any, used to meditate here.

There is also an unsubstantiated claim that the Prophet Muḥammad ﷺ stood on the rock before being lifted up in al-Miʻrāj. Although it is true he ascended to the heavens from al-Ḥaram al-Sharīf (al-Aqṣā Sanctuary) no evidence exists to verify from which specific spot he did so.

3. Bāb al-Silsilah (Chain Gate)

One of the 14 entrances, on the Western Wall of al-Ḥaram al-Sharīf (al-Aqṣā Sanctuary).

4. Bāb al-Salām (Tranquillity Gate)

Next to Bāb al-Silsilah on the Western Wall of al-Ḥaram al-Sharīf (al-Aqṣā Sanctuary).

5. Silsilah (Chain) Minaret

This minaret, like others around al-Aqṣā Sanctuary, was built on the foundation of the original minaret during the Umayyad period. The present minaret is the traditional Syrian square tower type. It was reconstructed in around 1329. This minaret was reserved for the best *muezzin* and it was from this minaret that the call for prayers began, followed by other minarets.

6. Bāb al-Matarah (Ablution Gate)

This entrance is almost in the middle of the Western Wall.

7. Bāb al-Qaṭṭānīn (Cotton Merchants' Gate)

Next to Bāb al-Matarah along the Western Wall.

8. Bāb al-Ḥadīd (Iron Gate)

Further along the Western Wall, and next to Bāb al-Qaṭṭānīn.

9. Bāb al-Nadhīr/Majlis (Council Gate)

The Awqāf has its office just outside the Bāb al-Nadhīr gates, along the Western Wall.

10. Minaret of Ghawānimah

This minaret took its name because it is next to the Bāb al-Ghawānimah. That gate was so called after the family, descendants of Shaykh Ghānim ibn 'Alī ibn Ḥusayn, who was appointed Shaykh of the Ṣalāḥiyyah Madarasah by Salāh al-Dīn. It was built around 1298.

11. Bāb al-'Atīm (Gate of Darkness)

This is the first entrance along the Northern Wall of al-Ḥaram al-Sharīf (al-Aqṣā Sanctuary).

12. Bāb al-Ḥiṭṭah (Gate of Remission)

This is the second entrance along the Northern Wall of al-Ḥaram al-Sharīf (al-Aqṣā Sanctuary) and it is used as the main entrance for people entering al-Ḥaram al-Sharīf (al-Aqṣā Sanctuary) from the northern side of the Old City.

13. Minaret al-Asbāṭ

This was constructed during the Mamluk era around 1367. This lies between the Bāb al-Ḥiṭṭah and the Bāb al-Asbāṭ along the Northern Wall of al-Ḥaram al-Sharīf (al-Aqṣā Sanctuary).

14. Bāb al-Asbāṭ (Gate of the Tribes)

This is the last entrance on the Northern Wall of al-Ḥaram al-Sharīf (al-Aqṣā Sanctuary).

15. Bāb al-Dhahabī (Golden Gate)

Dating back to the Umayyad times, the Golden Gate lies along the Eastern Wall of al-Ḥaram al-Sharīf (al-Aqṣā Sanctuary). The Golden Gate's two vaulted halls lead to the Door of Mercy, Bāb al-Raḥmān, and the Door of Repentance, Bāb al-Tawbah. Imām al-Ghazālī is thought to have written his Revival of the Religious Sciences – *Iḥyā' 'Ulūm al-Dīn,* while sitting and teaching above these gates. The Christians believe that 'Īsā ﷺ will, on his second coming, enter through this gate. While standing in the courtyard of al-Aqṣā Sanctuary to the right of the Golden Gate is Bāb al-Raḥmah (Door of Mercy) and to the left is Bāb al-Tawbah (Door of Repentance).

16. Cradle of 'Īsā ﷺ

A small niche in the ground at the extreme southeast corner of al-Ḥaram al-Sharīf (al-Aqṣā Sanctuary) above the Muṣalla Marwānī.

17. Muṣallā Marwānī (Solomon's Stables – substructure)

Just below the paved courtyard in the southeast corner of the al-Ḥaram al-Sharīf (al-Aqṣā Sanctuary) lies the vast vaulted subterranean area referred to, mistakenly, as Solomon's Stables. The actual construction is Umayyad dating back to the 8th Century. This area is accessible via a flight of stairs leading down to a recently renovated prayer area.

18. Islamic Museum

An extensive Qur'ān collection and Islamic ceramics, coins and glassware stand together with guns, swords and daggers in the oldest museum in al-Quds (Jerusalem). A unique group of architectural elements help document the history of al-Aqṣā Sanctuary.

19. Fakhriyah Minaret

This minaret lies at the junction of the Southern Wall and Western Wall. The exact date of this minaret's construction is difficult to ascertain, but it was definitely built in the Mamluk era some time between 1345 and 1496 CE (745-901 AH). The minaret was completely re-built during the Ottoman period and the muezzin's gallery renewed in 1920.

20. Dome of Yūsuf Āghā

Positioned along the line of the entrance to the Masjid al-Aqṣā half-way between the Western Wall and the Masjid al-Aqṣā.

21. Al-Burāq Wall (Western Wall, also called the Wailing Wall)

Jews today claim that al-Burāq Wall or "the Wailing Wall", which is an integral part of the western boundary wall of the Noble Sanctuary is all that remains of Herod's Temple. However, after a two year study, in 1931 a League of Nations Commission confirmed the following: "To the Muslims belong the sole ownership of, and the sole propriety right to, the Western Wall, seeing that it forms an integral part of al-Aqṣā Sanctuary, which is Waqf property. To the Muslims there also belongs the ownership of the pavement in front of the Wall and of the adjacent so-called Maghribi quarters opposite the Wall, in as much as the last-mentioned property was made Waqf under Muslim Shariah law, it being dedicated to charitable purpose".

22. Al-Kās (The Cup)

The place of ablution. This is between the Masjid al-Aqṣā and Qubbat al-Ṣakhrah (Dome of the Rock).

23. Summer Pulpit (also called Mimbar of Burhān al-Dīn)

Originally built in the 7th century, this open air pulpit is named after the 14th century Qadi of al-Quds (Jerusalem). Here Khuṭba for 'Īd and for special occasions was performed. This seems to have stopped some time in the 1600s.

24. Dome of Yūsuf

A dome built to commemorate Prophet Yūsuf (عليه السلام).

25. Dome of al-Naḥwiyyah (School of Literature)

Built in 1207 by al-Mu'aẓẓam 'Īsā as a school of literature.

26. Dome of Mūsā

A dome built to commemorate Prophet Mūsā ﷺ, built in 647/1249-50.

27. Fountain of Qāsim Pāshā

If you enter the al-Ḥaram al-Sharīf (al-Aqṣā Sanctuary) through Bāb al-Salām, immediately in front of you lies the Fountain of Qāsim Pāshā.

28. Pool of Raranj

To the left of the Fountain of Qāsim Pāshā, from Bāb al-Salām is the Pool of Raranj.

29. Fountain of Qayt Bey

Directly beneath this lies a vast cistern, which is the source of sabīl's water supply and said to have been an ancient gate passage. The present sabīl has been built over the original whose date is not known. The present sabīl carries a date of restoration made in 1883 by the Ottoman Sulṭān 'Abd al-Hāmīd. The original structure was constructed in 1453 by Mamluk Sulṭān Ināl.

30. Muezzin's Dome

If you enter al-Ḥaram al-Sharīf (al-Aqṣā Sanctuary) via the Bāb al-Matarah (Ablution Gate) and proceed to the Dome of the Rock, to the right of the flight of stairs is the Muezzin's Dome.

31. Dome of The Chain (Silsilah)

Directly east of the Qubbat al-Ṣakhrah (Dome of the Rock) is the Dome of the Chain, built by 'Abd al-Malik ibn Marwān. It marks the exact centre of al-Ḥaram al-Sharīf (al-Aqṣā Sanctuary).

32. Bāb al-Maghāribah (Moroccan's Gate)

This gate led to the Maghāribah quarters. This area was destroyed by the Israelis in 1967 and its inhabitants made refugees. The area is now accessible only to Jews and they have built a plaza there.

33. Dome of al-Nabī (Dome of the Prophet)

A dome built to commemorate the Prophet Muḥammad ﷺ. Restored in 1620 by Farūq Bey, the Governor of al-Quds (Jerusalem).

34. Dome of the Mi‘rāj (Ascension)

A dome built to commemorate the Prophet Muḥammad's ﷺ ascension. Restored in 1200; most probably built during the Ayyubid era.

35. Dome of al-Khalīlī (Hebronite)

An early 18th century building dedicated to Shaykh Muḥammad al-Khalīlī.

36. Miḥrāb 'Alī Pāshā

The Miḥrāb lies between Bāb al-Ḥadīd (Iron Gate) and Bāb al-Qaṭṭānīn (Cotton Merchants' Gate) along the Western Wall.

37. Dome of al-Khiḍr

A dome in the far north-west corner of the raised esplanade on which rests the Dome of the Rock. The dome is supported by 6 pillars.

38. Dome of the Rūḥ (Spirits)

Slightly to the left of Dome of al-Khiḍr as you face Masjid al-Aqṣā again, on the esplanade is the Dome of the Rūḥ supported by 8 pillars. This dome is frequented regularly by Sufis for dhikr.

39. Fountain of Sha'lān

Just to the right of the steps for the esplanade facing the Western Wall is an old brick structure, which was once used to supply water for the visitors.

40. Solomon's Dome

A dome built to commemorate Prophet Sulaymān ﷺ, built most probably during the Ayyubid era. Solomon's Dome lies to the right as you enter al-Ḥaram al-Sharīf (al-Aqṣā Sanctuary) via the Bāb al-'Atīm (Gate of Darkness).

41. Dome of the Lovers of the Prophets

A solid structure with large arches open on all sides. The Dome lies to the left as you enter al-Ḥaram al-Sharīf (al-Aqṣā Sanctuary) via the Bāb al-'Atīm (Gate of Darkness).

42. Fountain of Sulṭān Sulaymān

A rectangular column set in the ground just before the Dome of the Lovers, again as you enter al-Ḥaram al-Sharīf (al-Aqṣā Sanctuary) via the Bāb al-'Atīm (Gate of Darkness).

43. Sulaymān's Throne

Facing the Golden Gate, Sulaymān's Throne is on the left along the Eastern Wall.

44. Fountain of Ibrāhīm al-Rūmī

Built in 1435 CE for the sole purpose of giving water to the needy and travellers. It was built during the reign of Sulṭān al-Malik al-Ashraf. The fountain is placed in front of Bāb al-Nadhīr/Majlis (Council Gate).

Notes

1. Ḥaram means that which is sacred. An area, where even certain lawful things are forbidden. Acts like hunting, uprooting trees, violence towards humans except in self-defence and carrying weapons, are forbidden. The word is used as an exclamation in Arabic in reaction to both bad and good news, meaning "God have pity".
2. The place refers to the very first major fitnah that occurred regarding Prophethood, namely that of Musaylimah al-Kadhdhāb, who claimed Prophethood.
3. Graetz, *History of the Jews*, Vol. 1, p. 300.
4. *Encyclopaedia of Jewish History*, p. 47.
5. Josephus, *The Jewish War*, New York, Dorset Press, 1985, p. 332.
6. Theophanes, *The Chronicles of Theophanes*. Trans. Harry Turtledove. Philadelphia, Uni. of Pennsylvania Press, 1982, p. 11.
7. Butler, Alfred J, *The Arab Conquest of Egypt (and the last thirty years of the Roman dominion)*. Oxford, Oxford Uni. Press, 1978, p. 131.
8. Imām Tirmidhī rates this *ḥadīth* as *Ḥasan Ṣaḥīḥ*. He then lists the names of the Companions who have narrated aḥādīth about the coming of 'Īsā and the killing of Dajjāl at 'Īsā's hands. They are: 'Imrān ibn Ḥuṣayn, Nāfi' ibn 'Uyaynah, Abū Barzah al-Aslamī, Ḥudhayfah ibn al-Sayd, Abū Hurayrah, Uthmān ibn al-'Āṣ, Jābir ibn 'Abdullāh, Abū Umāmah al-Bāhilī, ibn Mas'ūd, 'Abdullāh ibn 'Amr ibn al-'Āṣ, Samurah ibn Jundub, Nawwās ibn Sam'ān, 'Amr ibn al-'Awf, Ḥudhayfah ibn al-Yamān.
9. The reason the Bishop of Jerusalem requested to surrender to Fārūq ('Umar) was to fulfil the prophecy of the scriptures, which predicted: "Rejoice O Jerusalem! Al-Fārūq will come to you and cleanse you". (See al-Ṭabarī, Vol. XII, pp. 196).
10. al-Ṭabarī, Vol. XII, p. 191, op. cit.
11. The sentence 'No Jew will live with them in Jerusalem' was a condition set by the Christians in order to maintain the status quo. The Christians were concerned that the Jews who had been banished might be allowed to return by the Muslims. 'Umar ﷺ, however, did allow them entry into Jerusalem as

and when they wanted to, thus bringing to an end 600 years of exile. Theophanes, *Chronicles, p.* 39. and Michael the Syrian state the Bishop of Jerusalem, Sophronius made a treaty with Umar ﷺ forbidding Jews to live in Jerusalem. See Donner, *Conquest, Note* 287, *p.* 322. Also see Andrew Palmer, *The Seventh Century in West Syrian Chronicles.* "... as (the Bishop) desired concerning their churches and their customs. They accepted the amnesty and the oaths concerning Palestine. The stipulation was made that no Jew might live in Jerusalem...".

12. al-Ṭabarī, Vol. XII, p. 192. Balādhurī states 17 AH. However, Bishop Sophronius who surrendered the city died in March 638. See Stratos note XII.
13. A document found in the Cairo Genizah reveals that the Jews asked 'Umar for permission for 200 families to settle in the town. As the patriarch opposed the action strongly, 'Umar fixed the number of the Jewish families at 70. From *Encyclopaedia Judaica* (Jerusalem), p. 1409. Keter Publishing House Jerusalem Ltd, 1972.
14. Theophanes, op. cit., p. 39.
15. Dāwūd's ﷺ *miḥrāb* is mentioned in the Holy Qur'ān. Ibn Kathīr in the translation of *Sūrah Ṣād* 38, 1 states, "And has the news of the litigants reached you? When they climbed over the wall into (his) *miḥrāb* (a prayer place)...".' (See Ibn Kathīr, op. cit.)

    As one faces the *qiblah* it was probably located to the far left of al-Aqṣā Masjid in al-Marwānī quarters or just beyond, where the earthquake of the Fatimid period claimed the land.
16. The *adhān* is said to have been called during 'Umar's ﷺ stay in Jerusalem. Bilāl ibn Rabāḥ the first *muezzin* in Islam (also called the Prophet's ﷺ *muezzin*) was, at some time, requested by 'Umar ﷺ to give the *adhān*. He complied even though he had vowed never to call the *adhān* after the Holy Prophet's ﷺ demise. When the Companions heard his inspiring voice vivid memories of the Golden Era in Madinah with the beloved Prophet ﷺ came flooding back and many were reduced to tears. Whether Bilāl gave the first *adhān* in al-Aqṣā Sanctuary or not is debatable.
17. In the centre of the Noble Sanctuary lies a huge rock on which some assume the Prophet ﷺ stood before making the ascension to the heavens. This entire Sanctuary was also the first *qiblah* of the Muslims. At the end of the seventh century, the Umayyad Caliph, 'Abd al-Malik ibn Marwān, ordered the construction of a 'Mosque' over the rock. The construction became one of the most beautiful features of Jerusalem. Today the skyline of Jerusalem glitters in the gold coloured Dome built over the rock.
18. al-Ṭabarī, Vol. XII, p. 197.
19. Estimates vary from 10 to 40 days.
20. 'Abdullāh al-Khatib, *British Journal of Middle Eastern Studies,* Vol 28 No1 May 2001, p. 30.

Appendix

QUR'ĀNIC REFERENCES

Direct references

17: 1

Indirect references

Holy Land/Blessed Land/Blessed Town:

5: 21
5: 22
5: 23
5: 24
5: 26
7: 137
21: 71
21: 81
34: 18

Honourable Place

7: 129

17: 4
17: 104
28: 5
28: 6
10: 93

Referred to as a town

2: 58
7: 161
7: 162
2: 259
34: 18

Referred to as a place & direction of Worship, Miḥrāb

17: 7
17: 4-8

Qiblah

2: 142 [140-150]
2: 143
2: 145
2: 146

Miḥrāb

3: 37
3: 39
38: 21

Symbolic Expression

95: 1

Seasonal Expression

106: 1-2

Stories of Prophets and People

Ibrāhīm عليه السلام

21: 71
37: 112

Dāwūd عليه السلام & Sulaymān عليه السلام

38: 18-20
38: 26
38: 30
21: 81
34: 12
38: 34
38: 35
38: 36
38: 37

Mūsā عليه السلام

2: 58
5: 21
5: 22
5: 26
7: 128
7: 129
7: 137
7: 161
10: 87
10: 93

17: 104
28: 6
34: 18

ʿĪsā ﷺ & Sayyidatunā Maryam

3: 35
3: 36
3: 42
19: 16
19: 22
19: 23
3: 45
3: 46
23: 50
3: 49
3: 55
4: 158

Narrations of Events

Before Islam

2: 114
2: 259
17: 4-7
106: 1-2

After Islam

17: 1
2: 142-150
30: 1-3

Ambiguous references

Places of Worship & Direction

2: 114
24: 36
10: 87

Site

23: 50

Eschatological events

50: 41
50: 44
57: 13

Index

‘Abbasid, 52
‘Abd al-Raḥmān ibn ‘Awf, 50, 87
‘Abdullāh ibn ‘Abbās, 50, 83
‘Abdullāh ibn Hawalah, 72, 74
‘Abdullāh ibn Salām, 50
‘Abdullāh ibn ‘Umar, 8, 14, 50, 68, 77, 83
Abū Bakr, 55, 56, 61, 76
Abū Dardā’, 50, 72, 76
Abū Dharr al-Giffārī, 50, 77, 85
Abū Hurayrah, 29, 30, 50, 57, 65, 71, 80, 83
Abū Mas‘ūd al-‘Anṣārī, 50
Abū ‘Ubaydaḥ ibn al-Jarrāh, 50, 86
Abū Umāmah, 69, 73
Acre, 52, 93
Adhān, 50, 51, 54, 91, 102, 137
‘Alī, 9, 68
‘Alqamah, 50
‘Amr ibn al-‘Āṣ, 50, 66, 83, 87
Anas ibn Mālik, 8, 77
Arāmiyah (Prophet), 15, 37, 39, 40, 41, 58
Aṭ-Ṭur, 64
‘Awf ibn Mālik, 50, 66
Awqāf, 117
‘Ayn Jālūt, 52

Bāb al-Asbāṭ (Gate of the Tribes), 119

Bāb al-‘Atīm (Gate of Darkness), 118, 133, 134
Bāb al-Dhahabī (Golden Gate), 120
Bāb al-Ḥadīd (Iron Gate), 116, 131
Bāb al-Ḥiṭṭah (Gate of Remission), 118, 119
Bāb al-Maghāribah (Moroccans’ Gate), 129
Bāb al-Matarah (Ablution Gate), 115, 116, 128

Bāb al-Nadhīr/Majlis (Council Gate), 117, 135
Bāb al-Qaṭṭānīn (Cotton Merchants' Gate), 116, 131
Bāb al-Salām (Tranquillity Gate), 114
Bāb al-Silsilah (Chain Gate), 114
Bāb al-Tawbah (Door of Repentance), 120
Barā' ibn 'Āzib Al- ﷺ, 13, 14
Bara' ibn Marur Al- ﷺ, 55
Bayt al-Maqdis, 13, 14, 54, 55, 56, 58, 68, 71, 73, 77, 79
Bilāl ibn Rabāḥ ﷺ, 50, 91
Bishr al-Ḥāfī, 51
Burāq Wall (Western Wall also called the Wailing Wall), 123

Charity, 76
Cradle of 'Īsā, 120
Crusaders, 52, 93, 94, 95

Dajjāl, 63, 64

Dāwūd (Prophet) ﷺ, 15, 16, 30, 31, 32, 33, 34, 36, 37, 84, 88
Dhahabī Al-, 66
Dhikr, 108, 132
Dhū'l-Nūn al-Miṣrī, 51
Dome of al-Khalīlī (Hebronite), 130
Dome of al-Khiḍr, 131, 132
Dome of al-Naḥwiyyah (School of Literature), 125
Dome of Mūsā, 109, 126
Dome of al-Nabī (Dome of the Prophet), 129
Dome of The Chain (Silsilah), 128
Dome of the Lovers of the Prophets, 133
Dome of the Mi'rāj (Ascension), 130
Dome of the Rūḥ (Spirits), 132
Dome of Solomon, 133
Dome of Yūsuf, 122, 125

Egypt, 3, 4, 7, 23, 25, 27, 28, 94, 100

Fārūq Al-, 86, 87

Fountain of Ibrāhīm al-Rūmī, 135
Fountain of Qāsim Pāshā, 126
Fountain of Qayt Bey, 127
Fountain of Sha'lān, 132
Fountain of Sulṭān Sulaymān, 134

Ḥabīb ibn Siba ﷺ, 50
Ḥadīth, 29, 51, 56, 63, 68, 72, 78, 79, 84
Ḥajj, 50, 82, 92
Ḥākim Al-, 66
Ḥasan al-Zuhrī Al-, 51
Heifer, 99, 104
Ḥiṭṭīn, 52, 94
Holy Sepulchre, 89, 92

I'tikāf, 77
Ibn 'Asākir, 66, 69, 75
Ibn Ḥajar al-'Asqalānī, 51
Ibn Qudāmah al-Maqdisī, 51
Ibrāhīm (Prophet) ﷺ, 6, 15, 23, 24, 25, 68, 69, 84
Iḥrām, 50, 82, 83
Imām Aḥmad, 8, 9, 63, 64, 65, 66, 68, 69, 71, 74, 75, 79
Imām al-Baghawī, 39
Imām al-Ghazālī, 51, 90
Imām al-Shāf'ī, 51
'Īsā (Prophet Jesus) ﷺ, 15, 39, 43, 45, 46, 47, 48, 49, 54, 57, 62, 63, 64, 120, 125
Islamic Museum, 121
Israel, 5, 25, 28, 37, 41, 46, 59, 97, 98, 99, 100, 103
Isrāfīl, 62

Jābiyah, 86, 87

Jibrā'īl, 54, 55, 57
Jihād, 71, 92, 106
Jund ibn Junādah ﷺ, 50

Ka'b al-Aḥbār ﷺ, 50
Ka'bah, 2, 10, 13, 14, 15, 22, 24, 25, 53, 54, 64, 77, 80, 84, 107
Kanz al-'Ummāl, 7
Kās (The Cup) – The place of ablution, 124
Khālid ibn Sa'īd ﷺ, 50
Khālid ibn Walīd ﷺ, 50
Khalīl (Hebron), 25, 90

Lake Tiberius, 94
Ludd, 62, 63, 64

Madinah, 4, 11, 13, 15, 18, 65, 73, 74, 75, 76, 77, 81, 86, 89, 90, 91, 106, 107
Mājūj, 62
Makkah, 2, 4, 10, 13, 14, 15, 18, 20, 21, 22, 24, 25, 53, 56, 57, 61, 67, 73, 76, 77, 78, 80, 81, 84, 85, 90, 92, 107
Mamluk, 52, 119, 122, 128
Mas'ūd ibn Aws ﷺ, 50
Maymūnah bint Sa'd ﷺ, 65, 79
Migration, 67
Miḥrāb, 131
Miḥrāb 'Alī Pāshā, 131
Minaret al-Asbāṭ, 119
Minaret Fakhriyah, 122
Minaret of Ghawānimah, 117
Minaret of Silsilah (Chain), 115
Mi'rāj, 53, 56, 57, 92, 109, 113
Mu'ādh ibn Jabal ﷺ, 50, 65, 71, 74
Mu'āwiyah ibn Abī Sufyān ﷺ, 50, 71
Muezzin, 128
Muezzin's Dome, 128
Muḥammad (the Prophet) ﷺ, 2, 4, 7, 8, 10, 14, 34, 50, 53,

54, 55, 56, 57, 63, 64, 67, 79, 81, 82, 90, 92, 105, 113, 129, 130
Mujamma ibn al-Ḥarith ﷺ, 63
Mūsā ibn Nuṣayr, 51
Mūsā (Prophet) ﷺ, 4, 25, 26, 27, 28, 29, 30, 104, 109, 126
Muṣallā Marwānī (Solomon's Stables), 121

Najd, 8
Nasā'ī, 2
Nawwās ibn Sam'ān Al- ﷺ, 62, 63
Nebuchadnezzar, 39, 87
Num'ān ibn Bashīr Al- ﷺ, 75

Ottoman, 52, 95, 122, 127

Pharaoh, 5, 6, 28
Pool of Raranj, 127

Qiblah, 10, 11, 14, 15, 89, 137
Qubbat al-Ṣakhrah, 91, 92, 93, 94, 102, 108, 113, 124, 128
Quraysh, 22, 56, 58

Sa'd ibn Abī Waqqāṣ ﷺ, 50, 83
Ṣaḥābah, 50, 51, 57, 90
Ṣaḥīḥ al-Bukhārī, 8, 14, 30, 34, 57, 58, 77, 80, 81, 85, 106
Ṣaḥīḥ Muslim, 56, 63, 66, 70, 80, 85
Ṣalāh, 2, 54, 78, 89
Ṣalāḥ al-Dīn al-Ayyūbī, 52, 94, 95, 101, 117
Salmān al-Fārisī ﷺ, 50, 107
Solomon, 35, 36, 133
Sayyidatunā Maryam, 15, 16, 17, 18, 43, 44, 47
Shaddād ibn Aws, 51, 106
Shām, 8, 106
Sharon, 101, 104
Shaykh Ghānim ibn 'Alī ibn Ḥusayn, 117
Shirkūḥ, 94
Sufis, 108, 132
Sulaymān the Magnificent, 113
Sulaymān (Prophet) ﷺ, 5, 6, 15, 33, 34, 37, 84, 109, 133, 134
Sulaymān's Throne, 134
Summer Pulpit (Mimbar of Burhān al-Dīn) 124
Sunan Abū Dāwūd, 51, 63, 65, 68, 69, 74, 79, 80
Sūrah Āl 'Imrān, 17, 18, 43, 44, 45, 46
Sūrah Al-A'rāf, 5, 27
Sūrah Al-Anbiyā', 6, 23, 35
Sūrah Al-Baqarah, 13, 19, 26, 40, 60
Sūrah Al-Isrā', 2, 4, 28, 38, 53, 59
Sūrah Al-Mā'idah, 5, 26, 27
Sūrah Al-Nisā', 47
Sūrah Al-Qaṣaṣ, 28
Sūrah Al-Rūm, 61

Sūrah Al-Ṣāffāt, 24
Sūrah Al-Tīn, 20
Sūrah An-Nūr, 19
Sūrah Maryam, 44, 45
Sūrah Qāf, 62
Sūrah Quraysh, 22
Sūrah Saba', 7, 31, 35, 36
Sūrah Ṣād, 16, 31, 32, 33, 35, 36, 88
Sūrah Yūnus, 27, 28

Ṭabarānī Al-, 70, 71, 72, 73, 76, 106Ṭalūt, 30
Tamīm al-Dārī ﷺ, 50, 51, 83, 90
Tartars, 52
Tawḥīd, 6
Temple Mount Faithful, 97, 101, 102
Tirmidhī, 2, 8, 63, 65, 69, 73, 77

'Ubādah ibn al-Ṣāmit ﷺ, 51
Umāmah al-Bāhilī ﷺ, 68
'Umar ibn al-Khaṭṭāb ﷺ, 50, 83
Umayyad, 52, 91, 92, 95, 112, 113, 115, 120, 121
Umm Salamah ﷺ, 82
Ummah, 14, 52, 54, 58, 82, 92, 101
'Umrah, 50, 82
'Uqbah ibn 'Āmir ﷺ, 50
'Uthmān (Caliph) ﷺ, 90

Ya'lā ibn Shaddād ibn Aws ﷺ, 51, 79
Ya'qūb (Prophet - Jacob) ﷺ, 25, 92
Ya'jūj, 62, 64
Yarmūk, 85
Yazīd ibn Abī Sufyān ﷺ, 50
Yūnus ibn Maysarah ﷺ, 74
Yūsuf (Prophet) ﷺ, 25, 125

Ẓāhir Al- (Caliph), 112
Zakariyā (Prophet) ﷺ, 15, 16, 17, 18, 39, 44